Proper Education Group

4 Practice Tests for the California Real Estate Exam

—

"The secret to getting ahead is getting started."
Mark Twain

Table of Contents

Introduction

1.1 Requirements

On the day of the test, you must bring the following:

1. A form of valid and not expired government-issued ID:
    a. Driver's license or DMV identification card
    b. United States Passport
    c. U.S. Military identification card

You are not required to bring a calculator. Basic calculators will be provided.

1.2 About the Exam

The test is 3 hours long and composed of 150 multiple choice questions. You must answer at least 105 of 150 questions correctly to pass the exam.

The exam is administered through a computer.

1.3 How to Apply

To apply for the exam, visit the website below, create your account and submit the required the forms:

https://www.dre.ca.gov/files/pdf/forms/re400a.pdf

All of the official documentation pertaining payments, documents, and forms can be found there.

1.4 Exam Results

Your score will be given to you immediately after finishing the exam.

Practice Test 1

Directions:

1.   You have 3 hours to complete the exam.

2.   To pass, you must answer at least 105 out of 150 questions correctly.

3.   Some questions will require mathematics. You may use a calculator.

4.   **Phones and pagers are not allowed. Having either will result in automatic dismissal from the exam and nullification of exam scores.**

Tips:

- Answer all questions even if you are unsure.
- Mark any questions you are stuck on and revisit them after you are done. The exam is timed so make sure you finish as many questions as you can.
- After reading the question, try answering it in your head first to avoid getting confused by the choices.
- Read the entire question before looking at the answers.
- Use the process of elimination to filter out choices that don't seem correct to increase your chances of selecting the correct answer.
- Be aware of important keywords like **not, sometimes, always,** and **never**. These words completely alter the ask of the question so it's important to keep track of them.

PLEASE READ THESE INSTRUCTIONS CAREFULLY.

Name: _____   Date: _____

1.	Ⓐ Ⓑ Ⓒ Ⓓ	31.	Ⓐ Ⓑ Ⓒ Ⓓ	61.	Ⓐ Ⓑ Ⓒ Ⓓ
2.	Ⓐ Ⓑ Ⓒ Ⓓ	32.	Ⓐ Ⓑ Ⓒ Ⓓ	62.	Ⓐ Ⓑ Ⓒ Ⓓ
3.	Ⓐ Ⓑ Ⓒ Ⓓ	33.	Ⓐ Ⓑ Ⓒ Ⓓ	63.	Ⓐ Ⓑ Ⓒ Ⓓ
4.	Ⓐ Ⓑ Ⓒ Ⓓ	34.	Ⓐ Ⓑ Ⓒ Ⓓ	64.	Ⓐ Ⓑ Ⓒ Ⓓ
5.	Ⓐ Ⓑ Ⓒ Ⓓ	35.	Ⓐ Ⓑ Ⓒ Ⓓ	65.	Ⓐ Ⓑ Ⓒ Ⓓ
6.	Ⓐ Ⓑ Ⓒ Ⓓ	36.	Ⓐ Ⓑ Ⓒ Ⓓ	66.	Ⓐ Ⓑ Ⓒ Ⓓ
7.	Ⓐ Ⓑ Ⓒ Ⓓ	37.	Ⓐ Ⓑ Ⓒ Ⓓ	67.	Ⓐ Ⓑ Ⓒ Ⓓ
8.	Ⓐ Ⓑ Ⓒ Ⓓ	38.	Ⓐ Ⓑ Ⓒ Ⓓ	68.	Ⓐ Ⓑ Ⓒ Ⓓ
9.	Ⓐ Ⓑ Ⓒ Ⓓ	39.	Ⓐ Ⓑ Ⓒ Ⓓ	69.	Ⓐ Ⓑ Ⓒ Ⓓ
10.	Ⓐ Ⓑ Ⓒ Ⓓ	40.	Ⓐ Ⓑ Ⓒ Ⓓ	70.	Ⓐ Ⓑ Ⓒ Ⓓ
11.	Ⓐ Ⓑ Ⓒ Ⓓ	41.	Ⓐ Ⓑ Ⓒ Ⓓ	71.	Ⓐ Ⓑ Ⓒ Ⓓ
12.	Ⓐ Ⓑ Ⓒ Ⓓ	42.	Ⓐ Ⓑ Ⓒ Ⓓ	72.	Ⓐ Ⓑ Ⓒ Ⓓ
13.	Ⓐ Ⓑ Ⓒ Ⓓ	43.	Ⓐ Ⓑ Ⓒ Ⓓ	73.	Ⓐ Ⓑ Ⓒ Ⓓ
14.	Ⓐ Ⓑ Ⓒ Ⓓ	44.	Ⓐ Ⓑ Ⓒ Ⓓ	74.	Ⓐ Ⓑ Ⓒ Ⓓ
15.	Ⓐ Ⓑ Ⓒ Ⓓ	45.	Ⓐ Ⓑ Ⓒ Ⓓ	75.	Ⓐ Ⓑ Ⓒ Ⓓ
16.	Ⓐ Ⓑ Ⓒ Ⓓ	46.	Ⓐ Ⓑ Ⓒ Ⓓ	76.	Ⓐ Ⓑ Ⓒ Ⓓ
17	Ⓐ Ⓑ Ⓒ Ⓓ	47.	Ⓐ Ⓑ Ⓒ Ⓓ	77.	Ⓐ Ⓑ Ⓒ Ⓓ
18.	Ⓐ Ⓑ Ⓒ Ⓓ	48.	Ⓐ Ⓑ Ⓒ Ⓓ	78.	Ⓐ Ⓑ Ⓒ Ⓓ
19.	Ⓐ Ⓑ Ⓒ Ⓓ	49.	Ⓐ Ⓑ Ⓒ Ⓓ	79.	Ⓐ Ⓑ Ⓒ Ⓓ
20.	Ⓐ Ⓑ Ⓒ Ⓓ	50.	Ⓐ Ⓑ Ⓒ Ⓓ	80.	Ⓐ Ⓑ Ⓒ Ⓓ
21.	Ⓐ Ⓑ Ⓒ Ⓓ	51.	Ⓐ Ⓑ Ⓒ Ⓓ	81.	Ⓐ Ⓑ Ⓒ Ⓓ
22.	Ⓐ Ⓑ Ⓒ Ⓓ	52.	Ⓐ Ⓑ Ⓒ Ⓓ	82.	Ⓐ Ⓑ Ⓒ Ⓓ
23.	Ⓐ Ⓑ Ⓒ Ⓓ	53.	Ⓐ Ⓑ Ⓒ Ⓓ	83.	Ⓐ Ⓑ Ⓒ Ⓓ
24.	Ⓐ Ⓑ Ⓒ Ⓓ	54.	Ⓐ Ⓑ Ⓒ Ⓓ	84.	Ⓐ Ⓑ Ⓒ Ⓓ
25.	Ⓐ Ⓑ Ⓒ Ⓓ	55.	Ⓐ Ⓑ Ⓒ Ⓓ	85.	Ⓐ Ⓑ Ⓒ Ⓓ
26.	Ⓐ Ⓑ Ⓒ Ⓓ	56.	Ⓐ Ⓑ Ⓒ Ⓓ	86.	Ⓐ Ⓑ Ⓒ Ⓓ
27.	Ⓐ Ⓑ Ⓒ Ⓓ	57.	Ⓐ Ⓑ Ⓒ Ⓓ	87.	Ⓐ Ⓑ Ⓒ Ⓓ
28.	Ⓐ Ⓑ Ⓒ Ⓓ	58.	Ⓐ Ⓑ Ⓒ Ⓓ	88.	Ⓐ Ⓑ Ⓒ Ⓓ
29.	Ⓐ Ⓑ Ⓒ Ⓓ	59.	Ⓐ Ⓑ Ⓒ Ⓓ	89.	Ⓐ Ⓑ Ⓒ Ⓓ
30.	Ⓐ Ⓑ Ⓒ Ⓓ	60.	Ⓐ Ⓑ Ⓒ Ⓓ	90.	Ⓐ Ⓑ Ⓒ Ⓓ

Name: _____   Date: _____

91.	Ⓐ	Ⓑ	Ⓒ	Ⓓ	121.	Ⓐ	Ⓑ	Ⓒ	Ⓓ
92.	Ⓐ	Ⓑ	Ⓒ	Ⓓ	122.	Ⓐ	Ⓑ	Ⓒ	Ⓓ
93.	Ⓐ	Ⓑ	Ⓒ	Ⓓ	123.	Ⓐ	Ⓑ	Ⓒ	Ⓓ
94.	Ⓐ	Ⓑ	Ⓒ	Ⓓ	124.	Ⓐ	Ⓑ	Ⓒ	Ⓓ
95.	Ⓐ	Ⓑ	Ⓒ	Ⓓ	125.	Ⓐ	Ⓑ	Ⓒ	Ⓓ
96.	Ⓐ	Ⓑ	Ⓒ	Ⓓ	126.	Ⓐ	Ⓑ	Ⓒ	Ⓓ
97.	Ⓐ	Ⓑ	Ⓒ	Ⓓ	127.	Ⓐ	Ⓑ	Ⓒ	Ⓓ
98.	Ⓐ	Ⓑ	Ⓒ	Ⓓ	128.	Ⓐ	Ⓑ	Ⓒ	Ⓓ
99.	Ⓐ	Ⓑ	Ⓒ	Ⓓ	129.	Ⓐ	Ⓑ	Ⓒ	Ⓓ
100.	Ⓐ	Ⓑ	Ⓒ	Ⓓ	130.	Ⓐ	Ⓑ	Ⓒ	Ⓓ
101.	Ⓐ	Ⓑ	Ⓒ	Ⓓ	131.	Ⓐ	Ⓑ	Ⓒ	Ⓓ
102.	Ⓐ	Ⓑ	Ⓒ	Ⓓ	132.	Ⓐ	Ⓑ	Ⓒ	Ⓓ
103.	Ⓐ	Ⓑ	Ⓒ	Ⓓ	133.	Ⓐ	Ⓑ	Ⓒ	Ⓓ
104.	Ⓐ	Ⓑ	Ⓒ	Ⓓ	134.	Ⓐ	Ⓑ	Ⓒ	Ⓓ
105.	Ⓐ	Ⓑ	Ⓒ	Ⓓ	135.	Ⓐ	Ⓑ	Ⓒ	Ⓓ
106.	Ⓐ	Ⓑ	Ⓒ	Ⓓ	136.	Ⓐ	Ⓑ	Ⓒ	Ⓓ
107	Ⓐ	Ⓑ	Ⓒ	Ⓓ	137.	Ⓐ	Ⓑ	Ⓒ	Ⓓ
108.	Ⓐ	Ⓑ	Ⓒ	Ⓓ	138.	Ⓐ	Ⓑ	Ⓒ	Ⓓ
109.	Ⓐ	Ⓑ	Ⓒ	Ⓓ	139.	Ⓐ	Ⓑ	Ⓒ	Ⓓ
110.	Ⓐ	Ⓑ	Ⓒ	Ⓓ	140.	Ⓐ	Ⓑ	Ⓒ	Ⓓ
111.	Ⓐ	Ⓑ	Ⓒ	Ⓓ	141.	Ⓐ	Ⓑ	Ⓒ	Ⓓ
112.	Ⓐ	Ⓑ	Ⓒ	Ⓓ	142.	Ⓐ	Ⓑ	Ⓒ	Ⓓ
113.	Ⓐ	Ⓑ	Ⓒ	Ⓓ	143.	Ⓐ	Ⓑ	Ⓒ	Ⓓ
114.	Ⓐ	Ⓑ	Ⓒ	Ⓓ	144.	Ⓐ	Ⓑ	Ⓒ	Ⓓ
115.	Ⓐ	Ⓑ	Ⓒ	Ⓓ	145.	Ⓐ	Ⓑ	Ⓒ	Ⓓ
116.	Ⓐ	Ⓑ	Ⓒ	Ⓓ	146.	Ⓐ	Ⓑ	Ⓒ	Ⓓ
117.	Ⓐ	Ⓑ	Ⓒ	Ⓓ	147.	Ⓐ	Ⓑ	Ⓒ	Ⓓ
118.	Ⓐ	Ⓑ	Ⓒ	Ⓓ	148.	Ⓐ	Ⓑ	Ⓒ	Ⓓ
119.	Ⓐ	Ⓑ	Ⓒ	Ⓓ	149.	Ⓐ	Ⓑ	Ⓒ	Ⓓ
120.	Ⓐ	Ⓑ	Ⓒ	Ⓓ	150.	Ⓐ	Ⓑ	Ⓒ	Ⓓ

1. When applying for a loan, what is a **fixed rate**?

   A. A loan that has a predetermined repayment interest rate
   B. A loan that has an interest rate that varies over time
   C. A loan that accrues no interest
   D. A loan that pays off the interest before the principal

2. What act prohibits discrimination based on race or color?

   A. Fair Housing Act
   B. Civil Rights Act of 1866
   C. Civil Right Act of 1964
   D. Civil Rights Act Amendment of 1974

3. What is the financial document that contains a written promise to fulfill a certain payment?

   A. Invoice
   B. Promissory note
   C. Pro forma statement
   D. IOU

4. What is the term used to describe the act of replacing an existing mortgage with another?

   A. Refinancing
   B. Defaulting
   C. Foreclosure
   D. Reinvesting

5. Which is **not** an appurtenant right?

   A. Furnace
   B. Swimming pool
   C. Air conditioning
   D. All of the above

6. What is the name given to the banking option that allows a customer to deposit a specified amount for a predetermined period of time?

   A. Certificate of occupation
   B. Certificate of deposit
   C. Investment clause
   D. Mortgage

7. If a seller nets $225,000 after paying a 10% fee, what was the total he received?

   A. $202,500
   B. $224,990
   C. $250,000
   D. None of the above

8. What is the name given to the rate earned for borrowing or an investment per year?

   A. Rate lock
   B. Fixed rate
   C. Floating rate
   D. Annual percentage rate

9. Other than buying a home using traditional channels, what other methods can a prospective owner use to buy a home?

    A. Public auctions
    B. Tender
    C. Lease
    D. Escalation clause

10. What is the reviewing of a borrower's credit worthiness prior to loan approval?

    A. Buydown
    B. Pre-qualification
    C. Credit score
    D. Under qualification

11. What is the document that is used to transfer legal rights to act in the interest of a person?

    A. Disclosure form
    B. Power of attorney
    C. Pro forma statement
    D. Deed

12. What type of listing only guarantees commission for a sale within a specified period?

    A. Exclusive listing
    B. Net listing
    C. Single agency listing
    D. Multi agency listing

13. What type of brokerage mandates that the broker acts in the best interest of the buyer?

    A. Single agency
    B. Dual agency
    C. Multi agency
    D. Full service

14. What is the name of a transaction where both the buyer and seller are seeking the best deal?

    A. Real estate transaction
    B. Credit transaction
    C. Arms-length transaction
    D. Debited transaction

15. What is the name given to modification of billing calculation dates?

    A. Modified date
    B. Closing date
    C. Opening date
    D. Adjustment date

16. What is the name of the mortgage that is transferred by the seller to the buyer?

    A. Assumable mortgage
    B. Adjusted rate mortgage
    C. Fixed rate mortgage
    D. Floating mortgage

17. What is the contract that secures a future transaction?

    A.   Deed
    B.   Call option
    C.   Title
    D.   None of the above

18. What does an exclusive listing contract need to be considered valid?

    A.   A net listing
    B.   A commission rate of at least 6%
    C.   A specified expiration date
    D.   The signature of the grantee

19. What is it when another state recognizes your real estate license?

    A.   Transfer
    B.   Limited basis policy
    C.   Reciprocity
    D.   None of the above

20. Which of the following is **not** a fiduciary duty?

    A.   Accounting
    B.   Confidentiality
    C.   Obedience
    D.   Privacy

21. What are contingencies as used in real estate?

    A.   Conditions that must be met by both the buyer and the seller before closing
    B.   Conditions set by the government on buying a home
    C.   Conditions set by the bank in order to approve a loan for a mortgage
    D.   Conditions that must be met to avoid judicial foreclosure

22. Who is a co-borrower?

    A.   Any individual whose name appears on the loan document
    B.   Someone that borrows money at the same time with you
    C.   The mortgage broker that originates the loan for you
    D.   An individual that guarantees your loan

23. What is the name given to a loan taken out to finance construction?

    A.   Mortgage
    B.   Construction loan
    C.   Business loan
    D.   Personal loan

24. What is the name given to the inspection done by the buyer before closing?

    A.   Final inspection
    B.   Advertorial
    C.   Housing ratio
    D.   Final walkthrough

25. What is the name given to a mortgage whose interest rate does **not** change throughout the payment period?

    A. Adjustable mortgage rate
    B. Floating rate
    C. Fixed mortgage rate
    D. Bridge loan

26. What is defined as the percentage owned by the buyer after making a down payment?

    A. Housing ratio
    B. Debt to income ratio
    C. Loan to value ratio
    D. Floating rate

27. What is the cash on cash return of a $60,000 investment that generates $1,000 in monthly cash flow?

    A. 1.67%
    B. 2%
    C. 20%
    D. None of the above

28. What is the term used to refer to the responsibility one individual has for the acts of another?

    A. Vicarious liability
    B. Fixed liability
    C. Current liability
    D. Contingent

29. What is the name given to a form used to explain the role of an agent in a real estate transaction?

    A. Purchase agreement
    B. Accountability
    C. Assignment contract
    D. Agency disclosure statement

30. A number of brokers agreed on a set standard commission. What antitrust law are they guilty of violating?

    A. Commingling
    B. Price fixing
    C. Steering
    D. Discussing

31. Which government agency is responsible for determining the status of an independent contractor?

    A. Federal government
    B. Bank
    C. Department of State
    D. IRS

32. What is the nature of the title issued in condo ownership?

    A. Freehold
    B. Regular
    C. Deed
    D. Clear title

33. Mr. and Mrs. Johnson made a $350,000 profit on the sale of their primary home. How much do they owe in capital gains tax?

   A. $0
   B. $3,500
   C. $50,000
   D. Half of the amount earned

34. What is the status of an agent's license once it is revoked?

   A. Pending
   B. Cancelled
   C. Breached
   D. Suspended

35. Which insurance policy provides extra liability coverage for the insured party?

   A. Umbrella policy
   B. Home insurance
   C. Flood insurance
   D. Hazard insurance

36. What is never included in the process of valuation?

   A. Comparative Market Analysis
   B. Appraisal
   C. Location
   D. Condition of the house

37. What type of contract allows the parties involved to disaffirm without liability?

   A. Bilateral contract
   B. Implied contract
   C. Unilateral contract
   D. Voidable Contract

38. What fiduciary duty does a broker neglect by failing to disclosing the buyer's inability to afford a down payment?

   A. Obedience
   B. Disclosure
   C. Accountability
   D. Confidentiality

39. James and Peter co-own a property where they both have equal undivided interests and right of survivorship. What co-ownership agreement do they have?

   A. Tenancy in entirety
   B. Joint tenancy
   C. Tenancy in common
   D. Tenancy at will

40. What is an exclusive term to describe the lease entered when an individual buys shares from a housing corporation?

   A. Percentage lease
   B. Gross lease
   C. Net lease
   D. Proprietary lease

41. What is the state of having no legal effect?

    A. Enforceable
    B. Cancelled
    C. Void
    D. Terminated

42. How many square feet constitute an acre?

    A. 25,235
    B. 43,560
    C. 50,525
    D. 70,000

43. What is the set minimum amp for a new construction?

    A. 100 amps
    B. 150 amps
    C. 200 amps
    D. 250 amps

44. What is the debt-to-equity ratio on a mortgage valued at $1,000,000 with a loan of $750,000?

    A. 25%
    B. 50%
    C. 65%
    D. 75%

45. Who controls flood insurance?

    A. FEMA
    B. EPA
    C. CERCLA
    D. FHA

46. What is a detailed building plan that is needed before starting construction?

    A. Building design
    B. Execution plan
    C. Blueprint
    D. Authorized plan

47. What type of house insulation was banned due to the release of formaldehyde fumes?

    A. Foam boards
    B. Loose fill
    C. Vapor barriers
    D. UFFI

48. Which deed is used to transfer interest in real property?

    A. Executor deed
    B. Quitclaim deed
    C. Deed of trust
    D. General warranty deeds

49. Which formal agreement gives an agent the sole right to sell a property?

  A. Purchase agreement
  B. Floating rate
  C. Exclusive Right-to-Sell Agreement
  D. Bridge loan

50. A tenant is legally allowed to remove equipment previously installed to facilitate business operations before the expiry of a lease. Why is this the case?

  A. The equipment is considered trade fixtures
  B. The equipment belongs to the lease holder
  C. The lessor does not want it
  D. It was part of the lease agreement

51. What type of easement attaches rights to an individual rather than the property?

  A. Easement appurtenant
  B. Easement in gross
  C. Prescriptive easement
  D. All of the above

52. What is the name given to the lowest section of the roof that extends into the sidewalls?

  A. Board
  B. Eaves
  C. Joists
  D. Beams

53. Which two parties are responsible for determining the commission earned by the broker?

  A. Seller and agent
  B. Seller and broker
  C. Buyer and agent
  D. Buyer and seller

54. Why must a lawsuit be filed within a specific time after an occurrence?

  A. To prevent the criminal from getting away
  B. Lis pendens
  C. Credibility
  D. Statute of limitations

55. Chris borrows money to purchase a new home and gives the mortgage to the lender as security. What term can be used to refer to Chris?

  A. Mortgagor
  B. Mortgagee
  C. Broker
  D. Buyer

56. What type of lease does a tenant have when he is paying a percentage of gross sales in addition to the base rent?

  A. Proprietary lease
  B. Net lease
  C. Percentage lease
  D. Gross lease

57. Why was the Civil Rights Act of 1866 significant in real estate?

   A. It protected against racial discrimination
   B. It protected interests of women
   C. It protected children's rights
   D. It protected against ageism

58. Why was the Privacy Act of 1974 significant?

   A. It required agencies to publicize records to the Federal Register
   B. It required privacy of records
   C. It required federal government to operate without transparency
   D. It required credit information to be kept private

59. Why was the Fair Housing Act of 1968 significant?

   A. It prohibited agents from asking prospective buyers about income
   B. It prohibited discrimination when selling, financing, or renting of a property
   C. It created affordable housing for low-income citizens
   D. None of the above

60. Jack is trying to convince Mary to sell her property in her neighborhood because it is changing due to the influx of people of other ethnic backgrounds. What is he doing?

   A. Steering
   B. Discriminating
   C. Blockbusting
   D. Convincing

61. What is the name of an agreement that allows for conditions on a property?

   A. Contract
   B. Deed
   C. Lease
   D. Qualified fee estate

62. What is **redlining**?

   A. Refusal by lending institutions to grant loans based on race
   B. Refusal by lending institutions to grant loans to people with poor credit scores
   C. Refusal of lending institutions to grant loans based on the agency being used for a purchase
   D. Refusal of a lending institution to make a loan because the area is integrated or populated by culturally diverse people

63. What is a form of co-ownership that involves a husband and wife having equal and undivided interest in the property?

   A. Joint tenancy
   B. Tenancy in common
   C. Tenancy by entirety
   D. Tenancy at will

64. What is the act of a property reverting to the state on death of the owner?

   A. Escheat
   B. Encumbrance
   C. Easement
   D. Suing

65. If you have a loan of $150,000 with an 8% interest, how much do you pay in interest every month?

A. $1,000
B. $1,200
C. $5,000
D. $12,000

66. Based on their contract, a lender declares the entire balance of the loan due immediately due to default by the borrower. How is this possible?

A. Payday loans
B. Alternative financing
C. Acceleration clause
D. Lines of credit

67. What type of payment plan allows a borrower to make smaller payments in the early years of a mortgage with payments increasing over time?

A. Blanket mortgage
B. Graduated mortgage
C. Anomalous mortgage
D. Balloon mortgage

68. What kind of mortgage should you apply for if you are buying more than an individual unit or plot?

A. Graduated mortgage
B. Blanket mortgage
C. Balloon mortgage
D. Adjustable rate mortgage

69. A salesperson is presented with two offers on a listed property. One is above the listing price and another below, which offer should he present to the seller?

A. Both offers
B. The one above the listing price
C. The one below the listing price
D. Neither

70. What is the name of a transaction where a seller finances the whole sale or part of the sale of a property for the buyer?

A. Mortgage
B. Refinancing
C. Purchase money
D. Buydown

71. What is an assessment of the value of a property as of a specific date based on objective data?

A. CMA
B. Listing price
C. Tax value
D. Appraisal

72. Which toxic metallic element is found in old paint and water pipes?

A. Mercury
B. Manganese
C. Cadmium
D. Lead

73. What is the amount of space used to calculate the lease payments which includes the shared property's common and service areas?

   A. Rentable square footage
   B. Usable square footage
   C. Common areas
   D. Service areas

74. Which chemical compounds commonly used in coolants and refrigeration contribute to the depletion of the ozone?

   A. CFCs
   B. Tetrafluoroethane
   C. Anhydrous ammonia
   D. Greenhouse gases

75. Which of the following does liability insurance protect you from?

   A. House fire
   B. Injury incurred on property
   C. Flood
   D. All of the above

76. What is a deed used for?

   A. To transfer title rights
   B. An official document proving a bank has loaned money
   C. A pro forma statement
   D. A lien

77. What is the measurement used to show the volatility of a market?

   A. Absorption rate
   B. Fluctuation rate
   C. Inflation
   D. Purchase deviation

78. What is the relationship between a broker and their client called?

   A. Fiduciary
   B. Trustee
   C. Seller disclosure
   D. Subagent

79. What is the law of agency?

   A. Commissions that are collected from both parties
   B. A set of laws that apply to a person who acts on behalf of another person
   C. The ability to accept an offer on behalf of the seller
   D. An authorized agency selling another's property

80. A severance is defined as _____.

   A. Real property that is converted into personal property
   B. Anything that is attached to the property naturally or by a person
   C. A person that is acting under a power of attorney
   D. An agreement between a lender and a borrower in which the borrower pledges collateral on a loan

81. _____ is the increase in value that occurs when combining two parcels into one large parcel.

   A. Redlining
   B. Plottage
   C. Assemblage
   D. Due diligence

82. What is a traffic report?

   A. A list of property's a broker is selling at one time
   B. A list of property that have been listed for sale in a specified area
   C. The number of property's a licensed broker is managing
   D. A list of prospects who have inquired or visited the property

83. What is the purpose of the Real Estate Settlement and Procedures Act?

   A. Provide buyers and sellers with disclosures regarding settlement costs
   B. Protect licensed brokers and agents from abusive practices regarding settlements
   C. Ensure buyers and sellers have the ability to back out of settlements within 30 days
   D. Pursue lawsuits against licensed brokers and agents on behalf of the client

84. _____ is also referred to as panic selling or panic peddling.

   A. Redlining
   B. Blockbusting
   C. Amortization
   D. Easement

85. A liability that consists of smaller payments of interest and principal and a balloon payment on the loan maturity date is a _____.

   A. Term loan
   B. Fully amortized loan
   C. Partially amortized loan
   D. Balloon loan

86. When a real estate license is responsible for maintaining a client's property and maximizing the return on investment, the licensee is acting as a _____.

   A. Building manager
   B. Property manager
   C. Broker
   D. Rental agent

87. Which of the following is an example of agricultural real property?

   A. Farm
   B. Warehouse
   C. Condominium building
   D. All of the above

88. A _____ is a law that defines how property in specific geographic area can be used.

   A. National Association of Realtors
   B. Federal Reserve Board
   C. Zoning ordinance
   D. Fair Housing Act

89. What is the purpose of a real estate appraiser?

   A. Provide an estimate of a property's value based on selling price

   B. Provide a professional estimate of the property's market value

   C. Work with a borrower to provide the lender with an annual market value of a home

   D. All of the above

90. _____ measures the rental rates with the value of real property.

   A. Real estate broker

   B. Arbitration

   C. Gross rent multiplier

   D. Mortgagor

91. What is the approach that is used to appraise a home by comparing a property with other properties similar in size and condition in the same area?

   A. Sales approach

   B. Comparison appraisal

   C. Market comparison approach

   D. Market data approach

92. A _____ is a loan where the borrower pays a down payment of 20% and receives a loan of 80%.

   A. Non-conforming loan

   B. Conventional loan

   C. Real property agreement

   D. None of the above

93. A potential buyer has been denied a loan from a lender. The seller of the home allows the buyer to pay an agreed amount every month for ownership of the property. What is this type of agreement called?

    A. Contract for deed
    B. Rent to buy agreement
    C. Real property agreement
    D. None of the above

94. A real estate licensee makes a change to an original contract. They extend the closing date on a contract by 30 days. This change is called a(n) _____.

    A. Assumption
    B. Addendum
    C. Collusion
    D. Reconveyance

95. Which of the following is an example of adverse possession?

    A. A buyer forcibly buying a piece of property
    B. A tenant refusing to leave at the end of a lease
    C. Continuous use of a private road
    D. All of the above

96. Which clause protects an agent from a seller waiting for a listing agreement to end to avoid paying a commission to an agent?

    A. Survival clause
    B. Amendment
    C. Extension clause
    D. Protection clause

97. Which organization is the largest purchaser of home loans in the secondary market and serves to stimulate homeownership?

   A. Mortgage Bankers Association
   B. Federal National Mortgage Association (FNMA)
   C. Government National Mortgage Association
   D. The Mortgage Bank

98. What is the purpose of the U.S. Department of Housing and Urban Development (HUD)?

   A. To ensure everyone has access to fair and equal housing
   B. To provide low income families with home loans
   C. To create government funded homes
   D. To regulate the housing market in the United States

99. Who oversee that Federal Housing Association?

   A. The Senate
   B. Federal National Mortgage Association
   C. U.S. Department of Housing and Urban Development
   D. States

100. The Equal Credit Opportunity Act (ECOA) prohibits lenders from discriminating against _____.

   A. Gender
   B. Marital status
   C. National origin
   D. All of the above

101. Which of the following is a reason the California Department of Real Estate can suspend a license?

   A. Moving out of state
   B. Failure to comply with educational requirements
   C. Failure to practice real estate
   D. All of the above

102. If a broker's license is suspended, what happens to the salespeople employed by the broker?

   A. The salespeople's license is temporarily suspended
   B. The salespeople can conduct business as usual
   C. They are fired from the brokerage
   D. They must find another broker to practice under

103. How long is a real estate broker's license valid for in the state of California?

   A. 2 years
   B. 5 years
   C. 1 year
   D. 4 years

104. The _____ enforces real estate law in the state of California.

   A. Real Estate Commissioner
   B. State governor
   C. Attorney general
   D. State senators

105. Which fee simple estate ends when a specified event or condition occurs?

    A. Fee simple condition
    B. Fee simple determinable
    C. Fee simple defeasible
    D. None of the above

106. When one joint tenant sells their shared interest in a property, what type of tenancy does the new owner hold?

    A. Periodic tenancy agreement
    B. Fixed-term agreement
    C. Tenancy in common
    D. Tenancy at sufferance

107. _____ is the state government's ability to govern zoning, city planning, building codes, and health standards.

    A. Real estate law
    B. Police power
    C. Zoning laws
    D. Eminent domain

108. How much is the California homestead exemption?

    A. $75,000
    B. $100,000
    C. $150,000
    D. Both A&B

109. The _____ are the legal rights that are attached to the ownership of real property.

A. Bundle of legal rights
B. Real estate law
C. Police power
D. Property rights

110. A renter with a lease has what kind of estate?

A. Fee simple estate
B. Less than freehold estate
C. Freehold estate
D. Fee simple subsequent

111. Which of the following is not a requirement for a promissory note?

A. A legal capacity to contract
B. Paid to the bearer
C. In writing or verbally
D. Voluntarily delivered to the borrower

112. In the state of California, a loan is officially in default around day _____.

A. 120
B. 30
C. 60
D. 90

113. The right an owner has to all increase in equity of the property is _____.

    A. Equitable lien
    B. Equitable title
    C. Legal title
    D. Beneficial ownership

114. Which of the following is a party of a trust deed?

    A. Borrower
    B. Neutral party
    C. Lender
    D. All of the above

115. Which department regulates real estate in the state of California?

    A. Department of Real Estate
    B. Attorney General's office
    C. Department of Property Management
    D. Department of Property and Real Estate

116. Which type of estate can be passed by descent?

    A. Fee simple subsequent
    B. Estate of inheritance
    C. Freehold estate
    D. Tenancy in common

117. Who is required to sign a reconveyance deed?

    A.   A broker
    B.   A seller
    C.   A trustor
    D.   A trustee

118. The _____ is headed by the Real Estate Commissioner and is a real estate regulatory body.

    A.   California Real Estate Commission
    B.   California Bureau of Real Estate
    C.   Real Estate Law
    D.   Department of Real Estate

119. The commission's regulation 2270 states that _____.

    A.   Licensees who advertise online must indicate their license status
    B.   Internet advertising is not prohibited
    C.   Licensees must get approval for online advertising
    D.   All of the above

120. The most accurate source of information regarding real estate in the state of California can be found on?

    A.   California Department of Real Estate webpage
    B.   Attorney General's website
    C.   State department website
    D.   None of the above

121. Which statement is true about real estate advertisement?

    A. Only a broker can advertise real estate

    B. Both a salesperson and broker can advertise real estate

    C. An advertisement license must be obtained

    D. Anyone can advertise real estate services or product

122. Which of the following is true about California licensing laws?

    A. Must be 18 years of age

    B. Must complete the required courses

    C. Must complete an application

    D. All of the above

123. _____ applies to the use of the internet to advertise real estate in California.

    A. Commission's regulation 2270

    B. Commission's regulation 2100

    C. The Real Estate Advertising Act

    D. California Real Estate Laws

124. The CalBRE website provides which of the following to an examinee or licensee?

    A. Testing results

    B. Renewal of salesperson and broker license

    C. Exam schedules

    D. All of the above

125. Which of the following is not a qualification to become real estate commissioner in the state of California?

    A.   Serve as a real estate broker for a minimum of 10 years in any state

    B.   Serve as a broker for a minimum of 5 years in California

    C.   Have 5 years related experience in California within the last 10 years

    D.   None of the above

126. What is the purpose of section 10132?

    A.   Define a real estate salesperson

    B.   Define the acts requiring licensure and employment by a broker

    C.   Both A&B

    D.   None of the above

127. A person would like to apply for the real estate salesperson license. Which of the following must they submit to the State Department of Justice?

    A.   Driver's license

    B.   Fingerprints

    C.   Family history

    D.   Examination scores

128. How many hours of continuing education is required every four years to renew a license?

    A.   45 hours

    B.   60 hours

    C.   20 hours

    D.   80 hours

129. What is the grace period for license renewal in the state of California?

    A. 6 months
    B. 2 years
    C. 30 days
    D. There is no grace period

130. A licensee is going on a 2-month vacation prior to the required license renewal. They try to renew their license 70 days prior to the expiration date. Which of the following is true?

    A. Renewal can occur 90 days prior to the expiration
    B. The renewal must occur no more than 15 days prior to the expiration
    C. CalBRE will not accept the application for license renewal
    D. The renewal must be done on the expiration date.

131. _____ is an account that holds money from license and exam fees and is used for CalBRE operating expenses.

    A. Real Estate Education and Research Fund
    B. Real Estate General Fund
    C. Real Estate Recovery Fund
    D. California Real Estate Fund

132. What is the maximum amount that can be collected, per transaction from the Real Estate Recovery Fund?

    A. $250,000
    B. $15,000
    C. $25,000
    D. $50,000

133. Who has the authority to investigate actions of real estate licensees in the state of California?

    A.   Attorney General
    B.   Governor
    C.   Real Estate Commissioner
    D.   Any lawyer licensed in California

134. Which of the following statement(s) is(are) true regarding the California real estate license?

    A.   A licensee must collect payment regarding real property
    B.   Only a licensee can solicit listings of real estate or prospective tenants
    C.   A license is needed to negotiate real estate transactions
    D.   All of the above

135. The owner of a vacation property decides to sell his home. Which statement is true?

    A.   As the owner, they have a right to sell the property
    B.   The owner must have at least a salesperson license
    C.   The owner can only do it if they have a lawyer working on the sale
    D.   The owner cannot sell the property without a real estate licensee

136. Which of the following is not required to apply for a salesperson license?

    A.   Pass a written examination
    B.   Provide proof of legal presence in the United States
    C.   Have at least an associate's degree
    D.   All of the above is required

137. A salesperson who would like to become a broker must do which of the following?

    A.   Provide work verification to prove work as a salesperson
    B.   Be referred to by a broker
    C.   Have an associate's degree
    D.   All of the above

138. Which of the following is an alternative for the experience requirement of the real estate license in the state of California?

    A.   A licensed lawyer in the state of California
    B.   A 4-year university degree with a major or minor in real estate
    C.   A master's degree in business administration
    D.   There is not alternative

139. What are the requirements for a corporation to become licensed as a real estate broker?

    A.   Have an officer that is a qualified broker
    B.   Submit a corporation license application
    C.   Pay the fee
    D.   All of the above

140. How long must a licensee wait prior to applying for reinstatement of a revoked license?

    A.   90 days
    B.   2 years
    C.   1 year
    D.   6 months

141. A _____ is needed to supply prospective tenants with a list of prospective rentals in exchange for a fee.

   A. Salesperson license
   B. Prepaid rental listing service license
   C. Broker license
   D. A license is not required

142. When a real estate agent makes money off a sale on top of their commission paid by a client, this is called a _____.

   A. Secret profit
   B. Fraud
   C. Violation
   D. Arbitration

143. Which statement is true about the California real estate license laws?

   A. A person without a license can essentially act as an agent
   B. A person without a license cannot be paid to help a person buy a home
   C. A person without a license can be paid to help a person buy a home
   D. Both A&C

144. Which of the following is true about expired broker licenses?

   A. The broker must immediately stop licensed activity
   B. The broker's salesperson can continue to work with the broker's clients
   C. The broker's branch office licenses will be expired
   D. Both A&C

145. How many times can a licensee take the salesperson exam in the state of California?

    A.   4 times
    B.   12 times
    C.   As many times as they need to
    D.   1 time

146. Where can a person find information on the California Real Estate Examination test requirements and purpose?

    A.   California Business and Professions Code Section 10153
    B.   Through Google
    C.   California state website
    D.   None of the above

147. How does a person re-apply for the California Salesperson examination?

    A.   File a Salesperson Examination Application
    B.   Pay a fee
    C.   They do not need to re-apply
    D.   Both A&B

148. A potential buyer, a single mother with two kids, feels she has been discriminated against while searching for a new home. Where does she file a complaint?

    A.   California Bureau of Real Estate
    B.   Equal Opportunity Department
    C.   Department of Fair Housing and Equal Opportunity
    D.   Real Estate Commissioner

149. An agent falsely tells a buyer that the neighborhood they would like to buy a home in is deteriorating, and is not desirable. What is the agent doing?

   A. Blockbusting
   B. Steering
   C. Plottage
   D. Collusion

150. Which of the following is required to take private property through eminent domain?

   A. The property must be for public good or use
   B. The owner must have due process in the court system
   C. The property owner must be paid
   D. All of the above

Answer Key

1.	A	31.	D	61.	D	91.	D	121.	D
2.	B	32.	A	62.	D	92.	B	122.	D
3.	B	33.	A	63.	C	93.	A	123.	A
4.	A	34.	D	64.	A	94.	B	124.	D
5.	D	35.	A	65.	A	95.	C	125.	A
6.	B	36.	A	66.	C	96.	D	126.	C
7.	C	37.	D	67.	B	97.	B	127.	B
8.	D	38.	B	68.	B	98.	A	128.	A
9.	A	39.	B	69.	A	99.	C	129.	B
10.	B	40.	D	70.	C	100.	D	130.	C
11.	B	41.	C	71.	D	101.	B	131.	B
12.	A	42.	B	72.	D	102.	A	132.	D
13.	A	43.	A	73.	A	103.	D	133.	C
14.	C	44.	D	74.	A	104.	A	134.	D
15.	D	45.	A	75.	D	105.	B	135.	A
16.	A	46.	C	76.	A	106.	C	136.	C
17.	B	47.	D	77.	A	107.	B	137.	A
18.	C	48.	B	78.	A	108.	D	138.	B
19.	C	49.	C	79.	B	109.	A	139.	D
20.	D	50.	A	80.	A	110.	B	140.	C
21.	A	51.	B	81.	B	111.	C	141.	B
22.	A	52.	B	82.	D	112.	D	142.	A
23.	B	53.	B	83.	A	113.	B	143.	B
24.	D	54.	D	84.	B	114.	D	144.	D
25.	C	55.	A	85.	C	115.	A	145.	C
26.	C	56.	C	86.	B	116.	B	146.	A
27.	C	57.	A	87.	A	117.	D	147.	D
28.	A	58.	A	88.	C	118.	B	148.	C
29.	D	59.	B	89.	B	119.	A	149.	B
30.	B	60.	C	90.	C	120.	A	150.	D

1. **A) A loan that has a predetermined repayment interest rate**

Commonly compared to floating rate, which is a loan that uses external factors as a benchmark for interest rates and is usually fluctuating based on the external market.

2. **B) Civil Rights Act of 1866**

This act declares all citizens equal and under the protection of the law. The law emphasized protecting all citizens of African descent during the Civil War.

35

3.   **B) Promissory note**

This is a financial document by the issuer to the payee that contains a promise to make payment for a definite sum of money. It is usually valid for payment either on demand or on a specified date. It usually contains information regarding the principal amount, interest rate, date and place of issuance, maturity date and signature of the parties involved.

4.   **A) Refinancing**

This is the process of replacing an existing mortgage with another that offers more favorable terms to the borrower. Refinancing enables a borrower to negotiate for lower monthly payments, lower interest rates and renegotiate the loan payment term.

5.   **D) All of the above**

An appurtenance is real property fixed to the land that is passed along with the sale of a property.

6.   **B) Certificate of deposit**

This is a product offered by banks and credit facilities to customers enabling them to deposit a lump sum amount for a predetermined period with an agreed upon interest rate premium. Doing some research on the certificate of deposit terms offered by the different available facilities is important to yield better returns.

7.   **C) $250,000**

$225,000 / (1 - 0.1) = $250,000

8.   **D) Annual percentage rate**

This is the annual rate charged on a loan or investment. It is usually used to express the actual annual cost of funds over the lifespan of a loan or cash investment. As loan arrangements vary among institutions and the situation surrounding the loan, a standardized APR is set to protect borrowers from unreasonably high interest rates.

9.   **A) Public auctions**

Homes are usually put on auction due to default on a mortgage or property taxes. Buying a house at an auction is risky as it often does not give the buyer a chance to view the interior of the house. When buying a property at an auction, it is necessary to run background research on the property.

10. **B) Pre-qualification**

These is the process of reviewing clients' creditworthiness and is usually used as a marketing strategy to obtain new clients. Creditors usually mail a potential borrower outlining maximum limit for loan.

11. **B) Power of attorney**

This is a legal document that transfers rights to act in place of a principal in the event that they are unable to act for themselves. The terms of the contract usually include what can be managed and where the power of the agent ends.

12. **A) Exclusive listing**

An exclusive listing is an agreement between a seller and an agent stating that commission on a sale can only be earned when a sale is made within a specified period of time. The timeframe for the sale is usually agreed on by both parties while entering the agreement.

13. **A) Single agency**

This is brokerage agreement where a buying agent is assigned the role to represent a buyer and works in single agency capacity as the buyer's agent. This agent is bound by fiduciary duties to the buyer and cannot disclose any confidential information to the other party.

14. **C) Arms-length transaction**

This is a transaction where both the buyer and the seller are acting in self-interest with an aim of getting the better deal. The discrepancy is usually solved when both parties agree on a middle ground that fulfills the interests of both the buyer and the seller.

15. **D) Adjustment date**

This is the changing of a date where calculations on items such as property taxes, rent and damage deposits are done.

16. **A) Assumable mortgage**

This is a mortgage arrangement that allows the seller to transfer the terms and conditions of a mortgage to a buyer. In this case, a buyer absorbs the seller's remaining debt instead of taking out a new mortgage.

17. **B) Call option**

This is a contract signed by both the buyer and the seller giving one party the right to sell and the other the right to buy a property on a future date. The price of the property is usually included in the contract and remains the same regardless of inflation or market shifts.

18. **C) A specified expiration date**

An exclusive listing contract is an agreement where a real estate agent receives commission within a specified amount of time. The agent receives commission no matter how the buyer is found.

19. **C) Reciprocity**

Real estate license reciprocity allows agents to obtain a real estate license in another state by taking the reciprocal state's exam.

20. **D) Privacy**

The 6 fiduciary duties of a real estate agent are: **O**bedience, **L**oyalty, **D**isclosure, **C**onfidentiality, **A**ccountability, and **R**easonable care / diligence (OLDCAR)

21. **A) Conditions that must be met by both the buyer and the seller before closing**

They are set in place to protect the parties involved in the contract. A breach in the contingencies results in the immediate termination of the contract.

22. **A) Any individual whose name appears on the loan document**

This is often someone whose credit score was taken into consideration when determining whether or not a loan can be extended. A co-borrower can be beneficial for a borrower that is unable to get favorable interest rates.

23. **B) Construction loan**

This is a short-term loan that is usually taken to finance the construction of a home or real estate property. It is usually taken to provide cash flow before larger funding is approved.

24. **D) Final walkthrough**

This is a visit done to the property by the buyer after all financing has been secured. A buyer is required to visit the premise and establish whether all the things that were discussed in the contract have been met prior to closing the deal.

25. **C) Fixed mortgage rate**

This is a mortgage loan whose interest rate remains the same throughout the longevity of the loan.

26. **C) Loan to value ratio**

This is defined as the percentage of the home's value owned by the borrower after making a down payment. It is calculated by taking the mortgage loan amount and dividing it by the appraisal value of the property being bought. The higher the loan to value ratio, the less likely lenders are to agree to loans.

27. **C) 20%**

($1,000 * 12) / $60,000 = 0.2

28. **A) Vicarious liability**

This is a secondary form of liability where a superior is held accountable for the actions of his subordinates. In the real estate sector, vicarious liability arises when an agent hired by either the buyer or seller acts inappropriately. In this case, the client is held accountable for the misconduct of his agent.

29. **D) Agency disclosure statement**

This is a statement signed by both the seller and buyer prior to the real estate transaction. Its role is to disclose the role of the agent in the transaction. An agent can either be a broker for either the buyer or the seller, a dual agent or a sub agent. In order to enforce disclosure laws, some states have a disclosure form written into law.

30. **B) Price fixing**

This is a situation that arises where a number of real estate agencies that dominate the market agree on a set commission. Brokers are required by law to set their individual commissions where consideration to the market going rate is allowed. Choosing to agree on a set standard commission could result in the suspension of a broker's license. These laws were set in place to protect the buyers and sellers in the market.

31. **D) IRS**

The IRS uses the general rule that an individual can be classified as an independent contractor if the payer has the right to control the result of work and not how it will be done.

32. **A) Freehold**

Freehold title is a title given to a freehold property where the owner owns the unit and the land on which the establishment has been developed and anything that is erected on the land.

33. **A) $0**

According to the Taxpayer Relief Act of 1997, a married couple is eligible for exemption from capital gain tax on profits of up to $500,000. This can only be claimed provided the property is the primary home of the selling couple meaning they have been living there for at least 2 years. Therefore, Mr. and Mrs. Smith do not owe anything in capital gain tax.

34. **D) Suspended**

He can choose to wait for the suspension to be lifted or look for another broker. A license can be suspended due to violation of insurance laws, providing materially misleading information and fraudulent practices. A revoked can only be reinstated after one year with undeniable evidence of trustworthiness and ability to uphold the law.

35. **A) Umbrella policy**

An umbrella insurance policy is an excess liability policy that is often used as a fail-safe for assets and savings. It is mostly used by people that are at risk of being sued. Contrary to popular belief, an umbrella policy does not cover additional risk area but acts as an addition to an already existing insurance.

36. **A) Comparative Market Analysis**

Comparative Market Analysis is never used in valuation as it is based on the market value of similar properties whereas no two real properties are alike.

37. **D) Voidable Contract**

A voidable contract is a formal agreement between parties that can be rendered obsolete due to legal factors. Some of the factors that can result in a voidable contract being rejected are fraud, undisclosed facts and a breach of the contract. A voidable contract is always considered legal unless rendered unenforceable.

38. **B) Disclosure**

Fiduciary duties arise when an agency operates on behalf of a client. In this case the agent is legally mandated to act in the best interest of the client. When an agent fails to disclose facts that may influence the final decision of the client, he is in violation of the disclosure clause.

39. **B) Joint tenancy**

A joint tenancy is an arrangement where two or more parties agree to co-own a property with equal rights and obligations. Upon death of a partner, the property remains solely in the ownership of the surviving partner. A joint tenancy has to be entered at the same time through a deed. Joint tenancy has the advantage of avoiding legal battles after the demise of a partner but can be hard to settle in the event of a divorced couple.

40. **D) Proprietary lease**

A proprietary lease is a is an agreement that allows a shareholder in a housing corporation to live in a unit equaling their stakes in the corporation. A shareholder does not buy the property but shares in the corporation. In this case, the shares act as collateral on the lease.

41. **C) Void**

This means to be obsolete and have no enforceable terms. Parties to a void contract are not bound by its terms making the contract unenforceable.

42. **B) 43,560**

An acre is a standard unit for measuring land. An acre does not have to be square shaped but contains an equivalent of 43560 square feet.

43. **A) 100 amps**

The minimum is 100 amps as anything below that may not be able to sustain the electric needs of a home. Larger homes can have between 150 and 200 amps based on the type of electronic systems installed. Having a proper electrical distribution in the home will also avoid trips.

44. **D) 75%**

750,000 / 1,000,000 = 0.75

The debt-to-equity ratio is used to determine whether a buyer can afford a house or to refinance an already owned property.

45. **A) FEMA**

The Federal Emergency Management Agency focuses on promoting the need to work together to support citizens and fast respondents. Its goal is to ensure citizens build and sustain to prepare for and recover from calamities.

46. **C) Blueprint**

A blueprint is a reproduction of a technical drawing on a light sensitive sheet that is done using a contact printer. A blueprint is usually required to predetermine the design and pattern that is going to be followed in a construction.

47. **D) UFFI**

Urea Formaldehyde Foam Insulation was used for house insulation in the 70s due to its high thermal resistance. Testing in the lab showed that the insulation produced fumes that were toxic for humans and the environment leading to its ban in 1982.

48. **B) Quitclaim deed**

This deed can be accomplished without being sold. No money is involved in this type of transactions and is most often used to transfer real estate between family members, i.e. when an owner gets married and wants to add the spouse's name.

49. **C) Exclusive Right-to-Sell Agreement**

This is an agreement between a seller and agent granting the agent or firm the exclusive right to market and sell a property.

50. **A) The equipment is considered trade fixtures**

Trade fixtures are removable personal property that are installed in a leased space to facilitate business running. For one to be allowed to remove a fixture, it must be essential for the running of the business to not cause damage to the property and be removed before the expiry of the lease.

51. **B) Easement in gross**

The rights associated by the easement are irrevocable for the person granted. A transfer of the property to another individual through sale or inheritance does not warrant an automatic transfer of the rights to the new owner. This renders the easement of gross void.

52. **B) Eaves**

An eave is the lower edge of a roof that protrude or hangs over the building's side.

53. **B) Seller and broker**

The seller and broker are usually responsible for agreeing in the amount of commission that should be paid to the broker

54. **D) Statute of limitations**

The statute of limitations is a law that sets the maximum period of time parties involved in a rift have to initiate legal proceedings from the day of the occurrence of the event. The time allocated to offences differs according to the nature of the offence.

55. **A) Mortgagor**

A mortgagor is an individual that borrows money from a lender in order to purchase a property. The lending is based on the individual's credit score and collateral. A title must be handed to the lender as collateral for the loan.

56.   **C) Percentage lease**

A percentage lease is a type of lease where the tenant pays rent plus a percentage of any revenue earned while doing business on the property. This agreement significantly reduces the rent paid. The parties involved agree on a base point where percentage lease kicks in.

57.   **A) It protected against racial discrimination**

The Civil Rights act of 1866 banned racial discrimination in real estate and housing transactions. People of any race had equal rights as whites to buy, sell, or lease property.

58.   **A) It required agencies to publicize records to the Federal Register**

The Privacy Act of 1974 is an act that established code of fair information maintenance governing the collection, use and maintenance of individuals that is maintained by federal agencies. The act required the agencies to publicize the records in the Federal Register.

59.   **B) It prohibited discrimination when selling, financing, or renting of a property**

The 1968 Act prohibited discrimination based on race, religion, national origin, sex, handicap and family status of the sale, financing, and rental of housing.

60.   **C) Blockbusting**

This is the act of trying to manipulate tenants to sell or rent their properties at lower rates due to an influx of minority groups in a once segregated neighborhood.

61.   **D) Qualified fee estate**

This is an estate agreement that facilitates the grantor to propose a set of conditions. A breach in the condition limitation may result in termination of the agreement. A quality fee estate can also be based on the occurrence of a predetermined event.

62.   **D) Refusal of a lending institution to make a loan because the area is integrated or populated by culturally diverse people**

This usually occurs when a lending institution has a map of areas they would not like to initiate credit in. Potential property owners are denied mortgages despite great credit scores due to the location of the property they intend to purchase.

63.   **C) Tenancy by entirety**

Only married couples can enter this type of co-ownership where the property is jointly owned as a single entity. It facilitates right of survivorship and can be terminated upon death of spouse or divorce.

64. **A) Escheat**

A property can be reverted to the state if no claimants have come forth to claim the property or the available heir has been deemed legally unfit to be granted ownership. It is revocable once a legal heir claims the property.

65. **A) $1,000**

($150,000 * 0.08) / 12 = $1,000

66. **C) Acceleration clause**

This is a contract that allows a lender to require full settlement of an outstanding loan due to a breach of predetermined conditions.

67. **B) Graduated mortgage**

This is a fixed price loan that allows the borrower to make smaller payments on the loan in the earlier payment years and continues to increase gradually until the mortgage is paid off. It considers individuals who were otherwise not qualified for the higher rate to qualify.

68. **B) Blanket mortgage**

A blanket mortgage is a mortgage that covers two or more pieces of real estate. The real estate property is held as collateral. Individual properties can be sold without having to retire the mortgage. This insurance is usually taken when purchasing and developing land.

69. **A) Both offers**

The agent is required by fiduciary duties to present both the offers to the client. Choosing to present the higher offer to the client in order to reap higher commission from the sale is a breach of fiduciary duties.

70. **C) Purchase money**

This is a mortgage issued by the seller as part of a real estate transaction. This arrangement is usually reached when the buyer is not eligible for the traditional mortgage. A down payment is usually placed on the property as an order of the financial transaction.

71. **D) Appraisal**

An appraisal is an opinion usually given by a professional on the market value of a property. Properties usually require an appraisal is unique and market value of similar properties may not offer an accurate value of the property.

72. **D) Lead**

Lead is a periodic metal that was used in paint in the 1970s as it accelerated drying, maintained a fresh appearance and resisted moisture. Older plumbing systems used lead lines and water often corroded the material as it was transported to the consumer's taps. Use of lead in paint was discontinued as it was found to cause nervous system damage and stunted growth in children.

73. **A) Rentable square footage**

Rentable square footage is inclusive of the usable square footage and common areas. The price per rentable square foot is usually calculated using a pro-rata calculation based on the size of the space being leased.

74. **A) CFCs**

CFCs are nonflammable chemicals that are commonly used in aerosol sprays and industrial cleaning products. Once these chemicals are released into the atmosphere they rise into the stratosphere where ultraviolet rays from the sun break them down. This breakdown releases chlorine atoms that destroy ozone molecules therefore forming ozone holes.

75. **D) All of the above**

Liability insurance covers everything from house fires, injuries incurred on the property, floods, injured domestic workers, falling trees, and more.

76. **A) To transfer title rights**

The buyer and seller must both sign a deed to transfer the property's ownership.

77. **A) Absorption rate**

This is a ration of the number of properties that have been sold against the number of properties that are available for sale within a specified area.

78. **A) Fiduciary**

Fiduciary is the relationship between client and broker. An agent is the fiduciary of the client.

79. **B) A set of laws that apply to a person who acts on behalf of another person**

The law of agency is a set of duties that real estate professionals owe to their clients, including disclosures that must be made to the client. These duties are set by each state.

80. **A) Real property that is converted into personal property**

There are two types of severance, actual severance and constructive severance. An actual severance is when an item is removed from the land and a constructive severance is when an item is detached by intent.

81. **B) Plottage**

Plottage occurs when the total value of a combined parcel is worth more than the sum of the individual parcels. The process of combining the parcel is called assemblage.

82. **D) A list of prospects who have inquired or visited the property**

A traffic report keeps a count of prospective buyers who have called about or visited the property.

83. **A) Provide buyers and sellers with disclosures regarding settlement costs**

RESPA is a consumer protection act that provides procedures that need to be followed in one-to-four residential real estate sales. It assists in eliminating abusive practices during settlements, bars kickback and limits the use of escrow accounts

84. **B) Blockbusting**

An illegal act that is not permitted by the Fair Housing Laws. This method manipulates homeowners into selling or renting their home at a lower price by falsely stating that minorities (racial, religious, etc.,) are moving into a once segregated neighborhood.

85. **C) Partially amortized loan**

A partially amortized loan is a loan that involves partial amortization during the loan term and a lump sum on the loan maturity date.

86. **B) Property manager**

A property manager is responsible for maintaining a client's property and maximizing the return on the client's investment. When a licensee acts on behalf of a client and doing the above, they are acting as a property manager.

87. **A) Farm**

A farm is an example of an agricultural real property. Agricultural real property is property that is used for farming and can be the farmers real presence.

88.   **C) Zoning ordinance**

A zoning ordinance specifies which zones can be used for residential or commercial purposes. It may also regulate the lot size, placement, bulk and height of the structures.

89.   **B) Provide a professional estimate of the property's market value**

A real estate appraiser is responsible for providing an estimate of a property's market value. This is established by using appraisal methods and a trained, professional judgement.

90.   **C) Gross rent multiplier**

The gross rent multiplier is the ratio of the price of an investment property to its annual rental income. This ratio is prior to accounting for expenses like insurance, utilities, and property taxes.

91.   **D) Market data approach**

The market data approach, also called sales comparison approach, finds value of property by comparing it to other properties that are similar in size and condition. The properties are also in the same area. Appraisers will typically use comparable homes that were sold within 6 months of the appraisal.

92.   **B) Conventional loan**

In a conventional loan a borrower pays a down payment of 20% and receives a loan for the remaining 80%. There is not government involvement in a conventional loan.

93.   **A) Contract for deed**

A contract for deed or an installment contract is a simpler way for a buyer to buy a home. It is an agreement between the seller and the buyer that the buyer will pay a monthly payment to the seller and the deed to the home is turned over to the buyer when all payments have been made.

94.   **B) Addendum**

An addendum is a change made to an original contract. The addendum is also called an amendment.

95.   **C) Continuous use of a private road**

Adverse possession allows a person to claim a property right owned by another person. The person can gain the title by using another's property continuously, openly and without permission for a certain period of time. It is also called squatter's rights.

96. **D) Protection clause**

This clause entitles a real estate broker to a commission after the listing is expired or canceled. It is only valid if buyers have viewed the property.

97. **B) Federal National Mortgage Association (FNMA)**

The FNMA is a government sponsored enterprise that serves to stimulate homeownership. It is the largest purchaser of home loans and raises money to buy notes from lenders.

98. **A) To ensure everyone has access to fair and equal housing**

HUD is tasked with providing housing and community development assistance, and ensure everyone has access to fair and equal housing. The mission is to create strong, sustainable and inclusive communities and provide quality and affordable homes to everyone.

99. **C) U.S. Department of Housing and Urban Development**

The FHA provides mortgage insurance on loans that are made by FHA approved lenders. They insure single family homes, multi-family properties, hospitals and residential care facilities.

100. **D) All of the above**

The ECOA prohibits discrimination in lending due to race, color, sex, religion, marital status, national origin and age.

101. **B) Failure to comply with educational requirements**

A broker's license can be suspended by the California Department of Real Estate. Failure to comply with educational requirements, the violation of the law and conduct deemed unethical by the department are all reasons a license can be suspended.

102. **A) The salespeople's license is temporarily suspended**

If the broker's license is suspended, then the salespeople working under that licensee have their license temporarily suspended as well.

103. **D) 4 years**

The broker's license lasts for 4 years. The licensee must complete continuing education requirements to renew the license.

104. **A) Real Estate Commissioner**

The Commissioner has the power to enforce real estate laws to achieves maximum protection for real estate consumers. They oversee all licensees in the state of California and employees.

105. **B) Fee simple determinable**

A fee simple determinable is an estate that ends automatically when a specified event or condition happens. The interest reverts back to the grantor or the heirs of the grantor.

106. **C) Tenancy in common**

This type of tenancy is concurrent, and ownership of property is with two or more people. The owners hold an individual and undivided ownership interest in the property.

107. **B) Police power**

Police power gives the government the ability to enforce zoning, city planning, building costs and health standards. This power takes the power out of the hands of property owners and gives it to the state government.

108. **D) Both A&B**

The California homestead exemption is $75,000 for debtors under 65 and not disabled and $100,000 for debtors under 65, not disabled and living with at least one family member.

109. **A) Bundle of legal rights**

Owners have a bundle of legal rights that transfers to the owner with the purchase of the property. These rights include possession, control, exclusion, enjoyment and disposition.

110. **B) Less than freehold estate**

This type of estate is held by someone who is renting or leasing property. It is also known as leasehold estate and the key is the limitation of time.

111. **C) In writing or verbally**

A promissory note is a signed document that contains a written promise to pay a stated sum to a specific person. The promissory note also needs to be signed by a borrower and be payable on demand at a given time.

112. **D) 90**

A loan is officially in default around day 90 in the state of California. The California foreclosure process can last up to 200 days or more. Notice of trustee sale occurs after 180 days.

113. **B) Equitable title**

An equitable title is the person's right to obtain full ownership of a property or property interest. It is also used in conjunction with the term legal title which is the actual ownership of the land.

114. **D) All of the above**

All of the above are parties of a trust deed. A trust deed is a deed of conveyance that sets out and creates the condition of a trust.

115. **A) Department of Real Estate**

The Department of Real Estate is run by the real estate commissioner. It safeguards and promotes the public interest in real estate matters by overseeing licensure, regulation, education and enforcement.

116. **B) Estate of inheritance**

An estate of inheritance is the most complete form of property ownership. This type of estate can descend to heirs.

117. **D) A trustee**

A reconveyance deed is a document that releases the debtor from a mortgage. It states that the mortgage has been paid in full and the lender has acknowledged the full payment.

118. **B) California Bureau of Real Estate**

The CBRE administers the real estate license laws and manages advertising, funds, clients and customers. It is the regulatory body and is headed by the Real Estate Commissioner.

119. **A) Licensees who advertise online must indicate their license status**

This regulation states that a licensee needs to state their license status when advertising on the internet. It also states that false advertising can result in criminal, civil and advertising penalties.

120. **A) California Department of Real Estate webpage**

The website is the best and most accurate source of real estate information in the state of California. It provides information helpful for an examinee and a new licensee.

121. **D) Anyone can advertise real estate services or product**

A California license is not required to advertise real estate associated services or products as long as the services or products don't include any actions that requires a California license.

122. **D) All of the above**

California licensing laws require all of the above to obtain a real estate license. The licensee is also required to be honest.

123. **A) Commission's regulation 2270**

The commissions regulation are sets of rules. The 2270 is regarding the use of internet when advertising real estate in California.

124. **D) All of the above**

The CalBRE will provide all of the above to a licensee or an examinee. It is a tool for real estate personnel to use.

125. **A) Serve as a real estate broker for a minimum of 10 years in any state**

To become commissioner a person is required to have one of the following: 5 years of broker experience in which they are actively engaged in business in California or 5 years' experience associated with real estate activity in California within the last 10 years.

126. **C) Both A&B**

Section 10132 does two things; it defines the real estate salesperson and the acts that require licensure and employment by the broker.

127. **B) Fingerprints**

California requires a real estate applicant, for any license, to submit fingerprints to the State Department of Justice (DOJ).

128. **A) 45 hours**

To renew a real estate, license a licensee must complete 45 hours of continuing education every 4 years.

129. **B) 2 years**

A licensee has a 2-year grace period to renew their license in the state of California. To do so they must complete the required education, provide payment and fill out an application.

130. **C) CalBRE will not accept the application for license renewal**

CalBRE will not accept the application because it is being submitted more than 60 days in advanced. A licensee cannot renew their license more than 60 days prior to the license expiration.

131. **B) Real Estate General Fund**

This fund is an account that holds all the money that has been collected from license and exam fees. It is used for CalBRE operating expenses. 8% goes to the Real Estate Education and Research Fund and 12% goes to the recovery fund.

132. **D) $50,000**

The recovery fund can pay up to $50,000 per transaction and $250,000 per license to a claimant with a judgement against a real estate licensee.

133. **C) Real Estate Commissioner**

The commissioner can investigate anyone engaged in real estate activities. They also have the power to deny, suspend or revoke the license.

134. **D) All of the above**

All of the above is true about real estate licenses, all statements require a person to have a license. A license is also needed to offer to rent or lease property.

135. **A) As the owner, they have a right to sell the property**

The owner has the right to solicit for the sale of real property even if they don't have a real estate license. His legal representatives can also do this.

136. **C) Have at least an associate's degree**

A person does not need to have an associate's degree. They do however need to provide proof of legal presence, disclose criminal violations or disciplinary actions, pass a written exam and be at least 18 years of age.

137. **A) Provide work verification to prove work as a salesperson**

An employment verification is required to get a broker license. The license needs to work as a salesperson and must prove that they have done so.

138. **B) A 4-year university degree with a major or minor in real estate**

The equivalent experience verification states that a 4-year degree with a major or minor in real estate can be an alternative for experience requirement for a broker.

139. **D) All of the above**

California allows a corporation to become a real estate broker but in order to do so, an officer must be a licensed broker, an application must be submitted, and a fee must be paid.

140. **C) 1 year**

A licensee who has had their license revoked, needs to wait one year before they can apply for reinstatement of their license.

141. **B) Prepaid rental listing service license**

This license is required to supply prospective tenants with listings of residential property for tenancy. They are able to collect a fee for providing this service.

142. **A) Secret profit**

A secret profit is when an agent makes money on top of the commission. This usually refers to a situation where the property is sold to someone related to the agent.

143. **B) A person without a license cannot be paid to help a person buy a home**

California does not allow a person without a license to be paid a commission. A person without a license cannot accept compensation for representing someone in a real estate transaction.

144. **D) Both A&C**

The broker needs to stop all licensed activity and the broker's branch office licenses are cancelled. The broker's salesperson is also placed on non-working status and must stop all licensed activity. To reactivate the licensee must re-activate the broker's license, the salesperson's license and the branch office license.

145. **C) As many times as they need to**

California allows a person to take the salesperson exam as many times as it takes to pass the exam. The person may need to reapply in order to take the exam.

146. **A) California Business and Professions Code Section 10153**

This section provides information on the California real estate examination test and the exam's purpose.

147.   **D) Both A&B**

A person must re-apply for the salesperson examination every two years. In order to do this, they must fill out an application and pay a fee.

148.   **C) Department of Fair Housing and Equal Opportunity**

The DFHEO is charged with enforcing California's civil rights laws. They protect the people against unlawful discrimination in employment, housing and public accommodations.

149.   **B) Steering**

Steering is the illegal act of guiding home buyer to specific neighborhoods due to race, ethnicity or religion. The Fair Housing Act states that is unethical and violates the code of ethics.

150.   **D) All of the above**

Eminent domain is when the government (local, state, federal) takes private property for the public use. The government must pay compensation to the homeowner.

Practice Test 2

Directions:

1.   You have 3 hours to complete the exam.

2.   To pass, you must answer at least 105 out of 150 questions correctly.

3.   Some questions will require mathematics. You may use a calculator.

4.   **Phones and pagers are not allowed. Having either will result in automatic dismissal from the exam and nullification of exam scores.**

Tips:

- Answer all questions even if you are unsure.
- Mark any questions you are stuck on and revisit them after you are done. The exam is timed so make sure you finish as many questions as you can.
- After reading the question, try answering it in your head first to avoid getting confused by the choices.
- Read the entire question before looking at the answers.
- Use the process of elimination to filter out choices that don't seem correct to increase your chances of selecting the correct answer.
- Be aware of important keywords like **not, sometimes, always,** and **never**. These words completely alter the ask of the question so it's important to keep track of them.

PLEASE READ THESE INSTRUCTIONS CAREFULLY.

Practice Test 2

Name: _____   Date: _____

1.	Ⓐ	Ⓑ	Ⓒ	Ⓓ	31.	Ⓐ	Ⓑ	Ⓒ	Ⓓ	61.	Ⓐ	Ⓑ	Ⓒ	Ⓓ
2.	Ⓐ	Ⓑ	Ⓒ	Ⓓ	32.	Ⓐ	Ⓑ	Ⓒ	Ⓓ	62.	Ⓐ	Ⓑ	Ⓒ	Ⓓ
3.	Ⓐ	Ⓑ	Ⓒ	Ⓓ	33.	Ⓐ	Ⓑ	Ⓒ	Ⓓ	63.	Ⓐ	Ⓑ	Ⓒ	Ⓓ
4.	Ⓐ	Ⓑ	Ⓒ	Ⓓ	34.	Ⓐ	Ⓑ	Ⓒ	Ⓓ	64.	Ⓐ	Ⓑ	Ⓒ	Ⓓ
5.	Ⓐ	Ⓑ	Ⓒ	Ⓓ	35.	Ⓐ	Ⓑ	Ⓒ	Ⓓ	65.	Ⓐ	Ⓑ	Ⓒ	Ⓓ
6.	Ⓐ	Ⓑ	Ⓒ	Ⓓ	36.	Ⓐ	Ⓑ	Ⓒ	Ⓓ	66.	Ⓐ	Ⓑ	Ⓒ	Ⓓ
7.	Ⓐ	Ⓑ	Ⓒ	Ⓓ	37.	Ⓐ	Ⓑ	Ⓒ	Ⓓ	67.	Ⓐ	Ⓑ	Ⓒ	Ⓓ
8.	Ⓐ	Ⓑ	Ⓒ	Ⓓ	38.	Ⓐ	Ⓑ	Ⓒ	Ⓓ	68.	Ⓐ	Ⓑ	Ⓒ	Ⓓ
9.	Ⓐ	Ⓑ	Ⓒ	Ⓓ	39.	Ⓐ	Ⓑ	Ⓒ	Ⓓ	69.	Ⓐ	Ⓑ	Ⓒ	Ⓓ
10.	Ⓐ	Ⓑ	Ⓒ	Ⓓ	40.	Ⓐ	Ⓑ	Ⓒ	Ⓓ	70.	Ⓐ	Ⓑ	Ⓒ	Ⓓ
11.	Ⓐ	Ⓑ	Ⓒ	Ⓓ	41.	Ⓐ	Ⓑ	Ⓒ	Ⓓ	71.	Ⓐ	Ⓑ	Ⓒ	Ⓓ
12.	Ⓐ	Ⓑ	Ⓒ	Ⓓ	42.	Ⓐ	Ⓑ	Ⓒ	Ⓓ	72.	Ⓐ	Ⓑ	Ⓒ	Ⓓ
13.	Ⓐ	Ⓑ	Ⓒ	Ⓓ	43.	Ⓐ	Ⓑ	Ⓒ	Ⓓ	73.	Ⓐ	Ⓑ	Ⓒ	Ⓓ
14.	Ⓐ	Ⓑ	Ⓒ	Ⓓ	44.	Ⓐ	Ⓑ	Ⓒ	Ⓓ	74.	Ⓐ	Ⓑ	Ⓒ	Ⓓ
15.	Ⓐ	Ⓑ	Ⓒ	Ⓓ	45.	Ⓐ	Ⓑ	Ⓒ	Ⓓ	75.	Ⓐ	Ⓑ	Ⓒ	Ⓓ
16.	Ⓐ	Ⓑ	Ⓒ	Ⓓ	46.	Ⓐ	Ⓑ	Ⓒ	Ⓓ	76.	Ⓐ	Ⓑ	Ⓒ	Ⓓ
17	Ⓐ	Ⓑ	Ⓒ	Ⓓ	47.	Ⓐ	Ⓑ	Ⓒ	Ⓓ	77.	Ⓐ	Ⓑ	Ⓒ	Ⓓ
18.	Ⓐ	Ⓑ	Ⓒ	Ⓓ	48.	Ⓐ	Ⓑ	Ⓒ	Ⓓ	78.	Ⓐ	Ⓑ	Ⓒ	Ⓓ
19.	Ⓐ	Ⓑ	Ⓒ	Ⓓ	49.	Ⓐ	Ⓑ	Ⓒ	Ⓓ	79.	Ⓐ	Ⓑ	Ⓒ	Ⓓ
20.	Ⓐ	Ⓑ	Ⓒ	Ⓓ	50.	Ⓐ	Ⓑ	Ⓒ	Ⓓ	80.	Ⓐ	Ⓑ	Ⓒ	Ⓓ
21.	Ⓐ	Ⓑ	Ⓒ	Ⓓ	51.	Ⓐ	Ⓑ	Ⓒ	Ⓓ	81.	Ⓐ	Ⓑ	Ⓒ	Ⓓ
22.	Ⓐ	Ⓑ	Ⓒ	Ⓓ	52.	Ⓐ	Ⓑ	Ⓒ	Ⓓ	82.	Ⓐ	Ⓑ	Ⓒ	Ⓓ
23.	Ⓐ	Ⓑ	Ⓒ	Ⓓ	53.	Ⓐ	Ⓑ	Ⓒ	Ⓓ	83.	Ⓐ	Ⓑ	Ⓒ	Ⓓ
24.	Ⓐ	Ⓑ	Ⓒ	Ⓓ	54.	Ⓐ	Ⓑ	Ⓒ	Ⓓ	84.	Ⓐ	Ⓑ	Ⓒ	Ⓓ
25.	Ⓐ	Ⓑ	Ⓒ	Ⓓ	55.	Ⓐ	Ⓑ	Ⓒ	Ⓓ	85.	Ⓐ	Ⓑ	Ⓒ	Ⓓ
26.	Ⓐ	Ⓑ	Ⓒ	Ⓓ	56.	Ⓐ	Ⓑ	Ⓒ	Ⓓ	86.	Ⓐ	Ⓑ	Ⓒ	Ⓓ
27.	Ⓐ	Ⓑ	Ⓒ	Ⓓ	57.	Ⓐ	Ⓑ	Ⓒ	Ⓓ	87.	Ⓐ	Ⓑ	Ⓒ	Ⓓ
28.	Ⓐ	Ⓑ	Ⓒ	Ⓓ	58.	Ⓐ	Ⓑ	Ⓒ	Ⓓ	88.	Ⓐ	Ⓑ	Ⓒ	Ⓓ
29.	Ⓐ	Ⓑ	Ⓒ	Ⓓ	59.	Ⓐ	Ⓑ	Ⓒ	Ⓓ	89.	Ⓐ	Ⓑ	Ⓒ	Ⓓ
30.	Ⓐ	Ⓑ	Ⓒ	Ⓓ	60.	Ⓐ	Ⓑ	Ⓒ	Ⓓ	90.	Ⓐ	Ⓑ	Ⓒ	Ⓓ

Practice Test 2

Name: _____   Date: _____

91.	Ⓐ	Ⓑ	Ⓒ	Ⓓ	121.	Ⓐ	Ⓑ	Ⓒ	Ⓓ
92.	Ⓐ	Ⓑ	Ⓒ	Ⓓ	122.	Ⓐ	Ⓑ	Ⓒ	Ⓓ
93.	Ⓐ	Ⓑ	Ⓒ	Ⓓ	123.	Ⓐ	Ⓑ	Ⓒ	Ⓓ
94.	Ⓐ	Ⓑ	Ⓒ	Ⓓ	124.	Ⓐ	Ⓑ	Ⓒ	Ⓓ
95.	Ⓐ	Ⓑ	Ⓒ	Ⓓ	125.	Ⓐ	Ⓑ	Ⓒ	Ⓓ
96.	Ⓐ	Ⓑ	Ⓒ	Ⓓ	126.	Ⓐ	Ⓑ	Ⓒ	Ⓓ
97.	Ⓐ	Ⓑ	Ⓒ	Ⓓ	127.	Ⓐ	Ⓑ	Ⓒ	Ⓓ
98.	Ⓐ	Ⓑ	Ⓒ	Ⓓ	128.	Ⓐ	Ⓑ	Ⓒ	Ⓓ
99.	Ⓐ	Ⓑ	Ⓒ	Ⓓ	129.	Ⓐ	Ⓑ	Ⓒ	Ⓓ
100.	Ⓐ	Ⓑ	Ⓒ	Ⓓ	130.	Ⓐ	Ⓑ	Ⓒ	Ⓓ
101.	Ⓐ	Ⓑ	Ⓒ	Ⓓ	131.	Ⓐ	Ⓑ	Ⓒ	Ⓓ
102.	Ⓐ	Ⓑ	Ⓒ	Ⓓ	132.	Ⓐ	Ⓑ	Ⓒ	Ⓓ
103.	Ⓐ	Ⓑ	Ⓒ	Ⓓ	133.	Ⓐ	Ⓑ	Ⓒ	Ⓓ
104.	Ⓐ	Ⓑ	Ⓒ	Ⓓ	134.	Ⓐ	Ⓑ	Ⓒ	Ⓓ
105.	Ⓐ	Ⓑ	Ⓒ	Ⓓ	135.	Ⓐ	Ⓑ	Ⓒ	Ⓓ
106.	Ⓐ	Ⓑ	Ⓒ	Ⓓ	136.	Ⓐ	Ⓑ	Ⓒ	Ⓓ
107	Ⓐ	Ⓑ	Ⓒ	Ⓓ	137.	Ⓐ	Ⓑ	Ⓒ	Ⓓ
108.	Ⓐ	Ⓑ	Ⓒ	Ⓓ	138.	Ⓐ	Ⓑ	Ⓒ	Ⓓ
109.	Ⓐ	Ⓑ	Ⓒ	Ⓓ	139.	Ⓐ	Ⓑ	Ⓒ	Ⓓ
110.	Ⓐ	Ⓑ	Ⓒ	Ⓓ	140.	Ⓐ	Ⓑ	Ⓒ	Ⓓ
111.	Ⓐ	Ⓑ	Ⓒ	Ⓓ	141.	Ⓐ	Ⓑ	Ⓒ	Ⓓ
112.	Ⓐ	Ⓑ	Ⓒ	Ⓓ	142.	Ⓐ	Ⓑ	Ⓒ	Ⓓ
113.	Ⓐ	Ⓑ	Ⓒ	Ⓓ	143.	Ⓐ	Ⓑ	Ⓒ	Ⓓ
114.	Ⓐ	Ⓑ	Ⓒ	Ⓓ	144.	Ⓐ	Ⓑ	Ⓒ	Ⓓ
115.	Ⓐ	Ⓑ	Ⓒ	Ⓓ	145.	Ⓐ	Ⓑ	Ⓒ	Ⓓ
116.	Ⓐ	Ⓑ	Ⓒ	Ⓓ	146.	Ⓐ	Ⓑ	Ⓒ	Ⓓ
117.	Ⓐ	Ⓑ	Ⓒ	Ⓓ	147.	Ⓐ	Ⓑ	Ⓒ	Ⓓ
118.	Ⓐ	Ⓑ	Ⓒ	Ⓓ	148.	Ⓐ	Ⓑ	Ⓒ	Ⓓ
119.	Ⓐ	Ⓑ	Ⓒ	Ⓓ	149.	Ⓐ	Ⓑ	Ⓒ	Ⓓ
120.	Ⓐ	Ⓑ	Ⓒ	Ⓓ	150.	Ⓐ	Ⓑ	Ⓒ	Ⓓ

1. What is the process of attempting to recover a loan from a borrower that has stopped making payments?

   A. Concession
   B. Final walk through
   C. Foreclosure
   D. Private mortgage insurance

2. What fibrous material causes cancer when released into the air?

   A. Asbestos
   B. Cotton
   C. Textiles
   D. Trunks

3. What are the vertical beams that frame the house?

   A. Frames
   B. Joists
   C. Shingles
   D. Studs

4. What is a reason a broker may be suspended or have their license revoked?

   A. Misrepresentation
   B. Failure to retain clients
   C. Failure to sell property within specified timeframe
   D. None of the above

5. A property manager makes routine rounds to repair air conditioning vents. What is the term used to refer to this?

   A. Aesthetic maintenance
   B. Avoiding depreciation
   C. Preventive maintenance
   D. Proration

6. What is another term that can be used to refer to the lender?

   A. Seller
   B. Mortgagee
   C. Mortgagor
   D. Loanee

7. If a seller nets $150,000 from the sale of her home, and the commission is 4%, how much did the home sell for?

   A. $144,000
   B. $148,500
   C. $156,000
   D. $156,250

8. What is the name given to the restriction of land usage by the local authorities?

   A. Building codes
   B. Denial
   C. Land zoning
   D. Property tax

9. What is the lender required to do once it is a borrower is unable to clear a mortgage?

   A. Threaten borrower
   B. Sell property without court order
   C. Initiate judicial foreclosure
   D. Evict the borrower

10. Which association represents title insurance?

   A. American Land Title Association
   B. CERCLA
   C. Fair Housing Act
   D. FEMA

11. Which law was passed to regulate credit bureaus?

   A. Annuity law
   B. Consumer credit law
   C. Fair Credit Reporting Act
   D. Truth in Lending Act

12. What is the legal right granted to exit a property?

   A. Easement
   B. Escheat
   C. Right of egress
   D. Right of ingress

13. What is the name given to non-monetary investment?

   A. Sweat equity
   B. Investment
   C. Capital
   D. Maintenance

14. What type of arrangement allows a borrower to negotiate a lower interest rate?

   A. Buydown
   B. Mortgage
   C. Purchase money
   D. Purchase price

15. What is a title without any lien?

   A. Clear title
   B. Deed
   C. Freehold
   D. Regular title

16. What is the name given to the breakdown of an individual's credit history?

   A. Credit assessment
   B. Credit report
   C. Financial record
   D. Repayment report

17. What is another term used to describe ownership?

   A. Credit
   B. Equity
   C. Liability
   D. Shares

18. What is the notice filed against a borrower on missing the repayment deadline?

   A. Notice of cessation
   B. Notice to cure
   C. Notice of default
   D. Notice of intention

19. What is the name given to describe the period a lender must keep a loan offer open to the borrower?

   A. Due diligence period
   B. Loan repayment period
   C. Lock-in period
   D. Target hold period

20. Which of the following is a lease break?

   A. When a tenant breaks a rent prior to the date of expiry without a legal reason
   B. When a tenant terminates a contract once the lease has expired
   C. When a tenant breaks a lease with the agreement of the landlord
   D. When a landlord allows a tenant to sublease his residence

21. What is the term used to refer to a situation where the amount of funds required to meet an obligation are **not** available?

   A. Buydown
   B. Debt to income ratio
   C. Escrow
   D. Shortfall

22. What is the term used to describe a situation where taxes are reduced or completely scrapped to increase buyers in the market?

   A. Tax abatement
   B. Tax exemption
   C. Tax evasion
   D. Duty free

23. A property originally assessed at $500,000 appreciated at 4% the first year and then 5% the year after. What is its current value?

   A. $525,000
   B. $545,000
   C. $546,000
   D. None of the above

24. Which entity performs the percolation test?

   A. Department of State
   B. Building Inspector
   C. Homeowners Association
   D. Department of Health

25. If a property is taxed at 25% with a tax levy of $92,000, what is its assessed value?

   A. $65,000
   B. $115,000
   C. $122,666
   D. $368,000

26. What is the name given to a brief summary of the history of a title?

   A. Abstract of title
   B. Chain of title
   C. Deed chain
   D. History of deed

27. What material is used in construction to cover joints where two or more types of materials meet?

   A. Flashing
   B. Metal
   C. Wood
   D. Joint

28. What is the lowest section of the roof that overhangs beyond the sidewalls of the building?

   A. Eaves
   B. Joists
   C. Stud
   D. Shingles

29. Which real estate metric is found by dividing cash flow by the deposit and settlement costs?

   A. Cash out
   B. Cash on cash return
   C. Lock in period
   D. Loan to value ratio

30. Which board committee is responsible for maintaining the aesthetic view of a town?

   A. Architectural Review Board
   B. Federal government
   C. Municipality
   D. HOA

31. What type of lease is taken on a loft?

   A. Net lease
   B. Gross lease
   C. Percentage lease
   D. Proprietary lease

32. What clause can prohibit having loud parties?

   A. House rules
   B. Regulations
   C. Lease terms
   D. Noise permit

33. What is the measurement used to show the volatility of a market?

    A. Fluctuation rate
    B. Absorption rate
    C. Inflation
    D. Purchase deviation

34. What is the mortgage clause that allows a lender the right to demand immediate payment of a mortgage?

    A. Cancellation clause
    B. Acceleration clause
    C. Prepayment Penalty clause
    D. Release clause

35. Which agreement allows a property holder to cross another person's land?

    A. Easement appurtenant
    B. Easement in gross
    C. Prescriptive easement
    D. None of the above

36. Which of the following is insurance taken out as a protection against malfunctions associated with the acquisition of a new home?

    A. Flood insurance
    B. Homeowner's warranty insurance
    C. HO2
    D. Hazard insurance

37. What is it called when someone takes possession of a property without being the actual title holder?

    A. Acceleration clause
    B. Adverse possession
    C. Easement
    D. Escheat

38. What is a non-possessory interest in property or restrictive covenant burdening the title?

    A. Adverse possession
    B. Easement
    C. Encumbrance
    D. Escheat

39. What is the name given to the long beams that span the piers of a foundation offering support to the floor or ceiling?

    A. Eaves
    B. Frames
    C. Joists
    D. Studs

40. What conveys a grantor's interest in real property?

    A. Agreement
    B. Conveyance
    C. Offering the loan
    D. Title

41. What prohibits the solicitation of residential property listings?

    A. Commingling
    B. Non-solicitation order
    C. Regulation Z
    D. Termination of tenancy

42. What is exempt from property taxation?

    A. Colleges
    B. Office buildings
    C. Supermarkets
    D. Unoccupied land

43. Which fiduciary duty is violated by commingling?

    A. Accountability
    B. Disclosure
    C. Obedience
    D. Loyalty

44. What gives the government power to appropriate private property?

    A. Right of first refusal
    B. Riparian rights
    C. Eminent domain
    D. None of the above

45. What is the owner of a building prohibited to do regarding the disabled?

    A. Allow the disabled to be tenants
    B. Make the building accessible to the disabled
    C. Ensure they are treated like other tenants
    D. Refuse modifications for handicapped tenants

46. What act prohibits discrimination based on disability?

    A. The Americans with Disabilities Act of 1990
    B. Fair Housing Act
    C. Civil Rights Act of 1866
    D. Civil Right Act of 1964

47. What is the name given to a property tenure that can be terminated at any time?

    A. Tenancy in sufferance
    B. Terminated tenancy
    C. Tenancy in common
    D. Tenancy at will

48. If you have a loan of $350,000 with a 7% interest, how much do you pay in interest every month?

    A. $2,041
    B. $2,260
    C. $27,125
    D. $31,208

49. What law prohibits any type of discrimination on the basis of sex and gender?

A. Fair Housing Act
B. Civil Rights Act of 1866
C. Civil Rights Act Amendment of 1974
D. Americans with Disabilities Act

50. In 1988, the Civil Rights Act was amended to include?

A. Married women
B. Immigrants
C. Black people
D. Handicaps and familial status

51. What is the net income of a property valued at $500,000 and a capitalization rate of 14%?

A. $70,000
B. $43,000
C. $840,000
D. None of the above

52. What is the name of an appointed official who estimates the value of real property for taxing purposes?

A. Agent
B. Assessor
C. Appraiser
D. Tax official

53. What is the term used to describe a situation where a mortgage balance decreases due to periodic installments that pay down the principal and interest?

A. Adjustable-rate mortgage
B. Amortization
C. Lock-in period
D. Fixed-rate mortgage

54. What is an annual tax levied on the value of real property?

A. Capital gains tax
B. Real estate tax
C. Progressive tax
D. Regressive tax

55. What is the name given to a situation where an individual uses borrowed money to purchase a property?

A. Buydown
B. Purchase money
C. Leverage
D. Shorting

56. Which air conditioning system facilitates both heating and cooling?

A. Forced air system
B. Cooling system
C. Heating system
D. Thermostat

57. What is the waiting time for a real estate agent to renew a license once it is revoked?

A. Two months
B. One year
C. Five years
D. It is never reinstated

58. Who manages a co-op?

A. Board of directors
B. CEO
C. Co-op developers
D. Tenants

59. What is the value estimating process that uses similar available properties to determine the value of land?

A. Mirror method
B. Sales comparison method
C. Allocation method
D. Abstraction method

60. Who is required to sign a deed in a real estate transaction?

A. Attorney
B. Buyer
C. Grantor
D. Lender

61. What is a poisonous gas that comes from the breakdown of minerals in soil?

A. Ammonia
B. Chlorine
C. Helium
D. Radon

62. What are the rights of a person whose property is adjacent to or crossed by a river?

A. Exclusive rights to sell
B. Riparian rights
C. Rights of first refusal
D. Right of disclosure

63. What law requires full disclosure of all credit terms for consumer loans under the Truth in Lending Act?

A. Americans with Disabilities Act
B. Civil Rights Act
C. Fair Housing Act
D. Regulation Z

64. What is the name given to granting priority to an individual to buy or lease a property?

A. Bundle of rights
B. Exclusive right to sell
C. Right of first refusal
D. Right of possession

65. What is the loss of property value caused by economic or functional factors?

A. Economic obsolescence
B. Depreciation
C. Legal obsolescence
D. Aesthetic obsolescence

66. What kind of agent is a real estate agent?

A. Special agent
B. General agent
C. Dual agent
D. Subagent

67. What valuing method is Comparative Market Analysis **not** considered as?

A. Appraisal
B. Home valuing
C. Depreciation valuing
D. Tax returns valuing

68. What is a specific lien claimed by someone who has performed construction / repair / renovation work on the property and has **not** been paid?

A. Mechanic's lien
B. Involuntary lien
C. Mortgage
D. Judicial lien

69. What is the bottom piece of a frame that provides a nailing surface for the floor and wall system?

A. Eaves
B. Joist
C. Sill plate
D. Stud

70. What is a broker allowed to purchase for a real estate salesperson?

A. Phone
B. Medical insurance cover
C. Retirement plan
D. A company vehicle

71. When does a real estate salesperson first provide the agency disclosure form?

A. When the deal is about to be closed
B. After closing the deal
C. First substantial contact
D. Never

72. What is the definition of steering?

A. When you knowingly provide inaccurate information
B. Guiding families with children into an apartment building with other families with children and away from other buildings
C. Discriminating against people due to socio-economic status
D. Failing to provide proof of continuing real estate education

73. What is the value of a point on a mortgage?

    A.   1% of loan
    B.   5% of the loan
    C.   10% of the loan
    D.   50% of the loan

74. What type of talent are real estate salespeople?

    A.   Assistants
    B.   Independent contractors
    C.   Part time employees
    D.   Full time employees

75. What is the term used to describe a building that is separate from the main house?

    A.   Supplemental structure
    B.   Accessory building
    C.   Secondary land
    D.   Shed

76. The estate that provides absolute ownership of land is called?

    A.   Fee simple estate
    B.   Life estate
    C.   Conditional fee estate
    D.   Legal life estate

77. Which of the following is an example of community property?

    A.   Property that is inherited by the husband through marriage
    B.   Income that is earned by one spouse during the marriage
    C.   Income earned prior to marriage
    D.   A gift given to one spouse during the marriage

78. Fixture are considered _____.

    A.   Hypothecation
    B.   An agreement between the two parties
    C.   Items that are removable by the tenant before the expiration date of the lease
    D.   Real property

79. The commission that is due to a salesperson is decided by?

    A.   Chattels
    B.   State Law
    C.   Mutual Agreement
    D.   Court Decree

80. A real estate broker has become an agent of the seller when ____.

    A.   A listing agreement with the seller has been executed
    B.   They are responsible for sharing commissions
    C.   A broker acts in good faith
    D.   They are procuring cause

68 Practice Test 2

81. What is a promissory note?

    A.   An agreement between the mortgage company and borrower that shows the terms of the loan

    B.   A document that states the buyer's intention to buy a property for a specified amount

    C.   A note between the broker and buyer stating the exclusive-right-to-represent the buyer

    D.   An agreement between the seller and buyer providing a grace period for backing out of the sale

82. _____ occurs when a tenant vacates the property because the landlord failed to provide essential services.

    A.   Quit notices

    B.   Actual eviction

    C.   Constructive eviction

    D.   Notice to quit

83. A buyer has _____ to cancel a contract if a Seller's Disclosure Notice has not been provided prior to the effective date of the contract.?

    A.   9 days

    B.   7 days

    C.   30 days

    D.   A Seller's Disclosure Notice is not necessary for buyers

84. Which is not true about the Federal Fair Housing Act?

    A.   Prohibits discrimination in housing due to age

    B.   Protects people from discrimination when renting or buying a home

    C.   Prohibits refusal to sell or rent a house due to familial status

    D.   All of the above

85. When a property loses value because of the lack of maintenance on natural wear and tear it is called _____.

    A. External depreciation
    B. Physical deterioration
    C. Economic obsolescence
    D. Negative amortization

86. Which of the following is an example of an appurtenance?

    A. Light bulbs
    B. Sofa
    C. Refrigerator
    D. Parking space

87. What is a syndicate?

    A. When one party operates a real estate investment
    B. When a party creates a real estate investment opportunity
    C. When two or more parties create and operate a real estate investment
    D. When a party builds a residential home for their family

88. Which of the following is a bundle of rights afforded to the buyer of real estate property?

    A. Right of control
    B. Right of exclusion
    C. Right of enjoyment
    D. All of the above

89. Which of the following is not a physical characteristic of land?

A. Immobility
B. Indestructability
C. Square footage
D. Uniqueness

90. A _____ is personal property that is used in a business and can be removed by the tenant when the lease ends.

A. Escheat
B. Trade fixtures
C. Plottage
D. Redlining

91. The _____ replaced dower and curtesy.

A. Uniform Probate Code
B. Real Estate Licensing Act
C. Real Estate Code of Conduct
D. Real Estate Code of Ethics

92. What is the highest possible ownership that can be held in real estate called?

A. Fee simple absolute
B. Estate at sufferance
C. Defeasible
D. Estate at will

93. Which of the following is an example of an encumbrance?

    A. Student loans
    B. Deed restriction
    C. Mortgage
    D. All of the above

94. The _____ determines the water usage in states where the water is scarce.

    A. Property rights
    B. Riparian rights
    C. Doctrine Appropriation
    D. Littoral rights

95. Which of the following is an example of a prescriptive easement?

    A. Building a fence on a neighbor's property
    B. Using a part of a neighbor's property to access the side of a road
    C. A neighbor uses another neighbor's Wi-Fi
    D. All of the above

96. A _____ is an interest in real property that is limited to the duration of the lifetime of the owner?

    A. Life estate
    B. Appurtenant easement
    C. Deed restriction
    D. Lien

97. This organization buys, owns and operates real estate for investors.

   A. National Investment Trust
   B. The Real Estate Investment Association
   C. Fair Housing Association
   D. Real Estate Investment Trust

98. Which tax is based on the value of real and personal property?

   A. Ad valorem tax
   B. Property tax
   C. Real estate tax
   D. Investment property tax

99. A _____ is a fixed object that is used as a permanent reference point to mark landownership boundaries.

   A. Datum
   B. Monument
   C. Metes and bounds
   D. Nonhomogeneity

100. What is a chain or title?

   A. A history of ownership regarding a property's title
   B. A line from which elevations are measured
   C. A comparison of homes sold in the same area
   D. The right a broker has to collect commission even if the property is not sold

101. Which of the following is not a test to determine a fixture in real estate?

    A.   Intention of the party
    B.   Agreement between parties
    C.   Adaptability
    D.   History

102. A property owner's beach has disappeared from their beachfront home. What kind of damage is this?

    A.   Reliction
    B.   Riparian
    C.   Avulsion
    D.   Accretion

103. A property owner decides clear out trees from the 2 acres of land they own from their backyard. The owner is planning to sell the wood to neighbors as firewood. What process is the property owner using?

    A.   Cooperative
    B.   Severance
    C.   Chattel
    D.   Seisin

104. A buyer buys shares in a corporation that owns a property in exchange for the ability to live in said property. What type of housing is this?

    A.   Cooperative
    B.   Timeshare
    C.   Vacation home
    D.   Homeowner's association

Practice Test 2

105. Which of the following is an example of a fee simple defeasible estate?

    A. A buyer buys a house that has a condition in place stating that the original architecture features are never removed from the property

    B. A homeowner's association requires property owners to seek approval before making internal or external changes

    C. A seller requires a buyer to wait until the seller finds a new home to close escrow

    D. A buyer requires the seller to make specified changes prior to buying the home

106. A property owner tries to refinance his mortgage but has been notified that there is a lien on the property due to failure to pay property taxes. What kind of lien has been placed?

    A. Mechanics lien
    B. Involuntary lien
    C. Judgement lien
    D. Judicial lien

107. Which of the following is not a distinct form of ownership in the state of California?

    A. Voluntary tenancy
    B. Tenancy in common
    C. Joint tenancy
    D. All are forms of ownership in California.

108. A _____ is when an individual inheriting property gets a new tax basis equal to its fair market value at the time of the owner's death.

    A. Marital inheritance
    B. Double step-up in basis
    C. Property inheritance
    D. Right of survivorship

109. A _____ is when property is free of any liens or problems and can be easily sold.

    A. Lien free title
    B. Insurable title
    C. Marketable title
    D. None of the above

110. What type of system of land ownership is used in the United States?

    A. Personal property ownership
    B. Public property ownership
    C. Real property ownership
    D. Allodial system

111. _____ is the disclosure associated with property being subject to regular assessments that fund community improvements and services.

    A. Megan's law
    B. Mello-Roos
    C. Buyer's contract
    D. Listing contract

112. California law requires sellers to disclose details about the property that may affect a buyer's decision to buy. Which statement(s) is true?

    A. The seller can face penalties if they fail to disclose
    B. The disclosure must be in writing
    C. These details are also called material facts
    D. All of the above

113. Which document is used to disclose material facts in the state of California?

    A. Transfer Disclosure Statement
    B. Petition Application Supplement
    C. Trust Fund Non-Accountability Report
    D. Publication Request

114. Every home that is listed by a real estate agent is placed on the _____ unless it has been exempted.

    A. Zillow
    B. Multiple listing service
    C. Real Estate Listing website
    D. Trulia

115. The laws of agency apply to which of the following relationship(s)?

    A. Between brokers
    B. Between principal and agent
    C. Between broker and salesperson
    D. All of the above

116. Which form would a seller use to disclose a military site in close proximity to the property in the state of California?

    A. Transfer Disclosure Statement
    B. Supplemental Statutory Disclosure
    C. Exempt Seller Disclosure Form
    D. General Disclosure Form

117. Transfer disclosures are required in all cases except _____ in the state of California?

   A. When property is sold by the owner
   B. When property is sold to a corporation
   C. If property is transferred between spouses
   D. If property is transferred between any family members

118. Which statement is true about full disclosure of property on sale?

   A. It comes with a tax relief
   B. It is required between agents
   C. It enhances the value of the property
   D. All of the above

119. Which is the most common type of real estate agency?

   A. General agency
   B. Subagency
   C. Seller agency
   D. Special agency

120. What are the steps to completing the agency relationship disclosure process (in the correct order)?

   A. Agree, disclose, elect
   B. Elect, agree, disclose
   C. Disclose, elect, confirm
   D. Disclose, confirm, choose

121. A seller must disclose a death in the property if it occurred within _____.

A. 5 years
B. 3 years
C. 1 year
D. 2 years

122. In what time frame does a listing agreement have to be submitted to the MLS after the agreement has been signed?

A. Within 48 hours
B. There is no timeframe
C. Within 1 week
D. Within 24 hours

123. Which clause safeguards an agent's commission after the listing expires?

A. Carryover clause
B. Extension clause
C. Safety clause
D. None of the above

124. Which statement is true about listing agreement?

A. Listing agreement can only be submitted to one MLS
B. Listing agreements can be submitted to multiple MLS's
C. Listing agreements can be submitted to only 2 MLS's
D. Listing agreement must be submitted to more than 2 MLS's

125. Which listing agreement(s) allow(s) an owner to sell the property themselves and avoid paying the commission?

    A. Open listing
    B. Exclusive right to sell listing
    C. Net listing
    D. All of the above

126. Which of the following is a reason a listing agreement can be terminated?

    A. If the seller decides not to sell the home
    B. If the broker's license is invalid
    C. If the broker does not sell the home within 30 days
    D. All of the above

127. What does the Sherman act provide provisions against?

    A. Price fixing
    B. Market allocation
    C. Group boycotting
    D. All of the above

128. The _____ is a piece of California legislation that safeguards business establishments from discrimination?

    A. Equal Opportunity Act
    B. Anti-discrimination Act
    C. Unruh Act
    D. California Business Protections Act

129. The Real Estate Law does which of the follow in the state of California?

    A. It helps brokers with retaining clients

    B. Allows only brokers to receive commissions

    C. Provides resources to real estate agents

    D. All of the above

130. What is the definition of blockbusting?

    A. When licensees encourage homeowners to sell due to an influx of minorities

    B. When a lender refuses to lend in a specific area

    C. When an agent lies about a specific area to stop a buyer from buying a home there

    D. When an agent raises commission to buyers because of the socio-economic status

131. Which statement is true about foreclosures in the state of California?

    A. An agent cannot sell a foreclosed home

    B. A person cannot act as a foreclosure consultant without obtaining a Certificate of Registration

    C. An agent does not need a Certificate of Registration to act as a foreclosure consultant

    D. None of the above

132. Which of the following complies with anti-discrimination laws?

    A. Advertising based on race or religion

    B. Setting restrictive standards for specific tenants

    C. Advertisement designed to attract disabled people to property modified for their needs

    D. All of the above

133. Numerous agents collaborated together and decided not to sell to specific customers in a particular area. What are the agents practicing?

    A. Redlining
    B. Blockbusting
    C. Market allocation
    D. Discrimination

134. Which 1963 California law helped end discrimination by property owners and landlords?

    A. Equal Opportunity Act
    B. Rumford Fair Housing Act
    C. California Anti-discrimination law
    D. Unruh Act

135. Which of the following is an exemption of the Unruh Act?

    A. Senior citizen housing
    B. People of low socio-economic class
    C. Immigrants
    D. People who are not U.S. Citizens

136. A seller agrees to a sell their vacation home to a buyer only if the buyer agrees to buy the sellers primary home. This is called a _____.

    A. Arbitration
    B. Tie-in arrangement
    C. Redlining
    D. None of the above

137. A real estate agent must comply with the _____, which states people on this list cannot be called.

    A.   California solicitation laws
    B.   Anti-solicitation list
    C.   Do Not Call Registry
    D.   None of the above

138. _____ is a strategy that involves planting, nurturing and cultivating real estate leads.

    A.   Soliciting
    B.   Door-to-door prospecting
    C.   Referral chain
    D.   Farming

139. A prospecting email needs to include which of the following?

    A.   All emails addresses be hidden
    B.   An opt-out option
    C.   Reviews from previous clients
    D.   All of the above

140. A _____ is a document that agents send to potential clients who wish to sell their home.

    A.   Listing package
    B.   Listing presentation
    C.   Listing contract
    D.   Marketing plans

141. Which is the most common reason for a property's failure to sell?

   A. Location
   B. Property condition
   C. Overpricing
   D. Marketing

142. When an agent fails to communicate a new listing to the MLS, is it called a(n) _____.

   A. Exemption
   B. Prospecting
   C. Failure to market
   D. Pocket listing

143. Information on a piece of property in the state of California can be found at the _____.

   A. County tax assessor's office
   B. District Attorney's office
   C. CalBRE website
   D. Broker's office

144. What do plat maps do?

   A. A map of property that shows an aerial view
   B. Shows how land is divided into lots in each county
   C. Parcels of land that show boundary lines
   D. Maps a state by natural resources

145. _____ prohibits false advertising in the state of California.

    A.   Department of Marketing
    B.   Attorney General's office
    C.   California Bureau of Real Estate
    D.   California Business and Professions Code 17500

146. A(n) _____ means that a buyer has made an offer that the seller has accepted but is conditional upon certain criteria.

    A.   Contingent offer
    B.   Good faith offer
    C.   Conditional offer
    D.   Prospective offer

147. In which case can a good faith deposit be refunded?

    A.   If they buyer backs out of the deal
    B.   If the buyer and seller agree to cancel the deal
    C.   If the seller takes too long to proceed with the offer
    D.   A good faith deposit cannot be refunded

148. California gives a buyer _____ to obtain financing and decide whether to move forward with a home.

    A.   30 days
    B.   7 business days
    C.   2 months
    D.   21 days

149. An agent must deposit earnest money within _____ days in the state of California.

    A. 3
    B. 1
    C. 5
    D. 10

150. Who has the ability to modify an accepted offer?

    A. Buyer
    B. Seller
    C. Broker
    D. A&B only

Answer Key

1.	C	31.	B	61.	D	91.	A	121.	B
2.	A	32.	A	62.	B	92.	A	122.	A
3.	D	33.	B	63.	D	93.	B	123.	C
4.	A	34.	B	64.	C	94.	C	124.	B
5.	C	35.	A	65.	A	95.	B	125.	A
6.	B	36.	B	66.	A	96.	A	126.	B
7.	D	37.	B	67.	A	97.	D	127.	D
8.	C	38.	C	68.	A	98.	A	128.	C
9.	C	39.	C	69.	C	99.	B	129.	B
10.	B	40.	B	70.	A	100.	A	130.	A
11.	C	41.	B	71.	C	101.	D	131.	B
12.	C	42.	A	72.	B	102.	C	132.	C
13.	A	43.	A	73.	A	103.	B	133.	C
14.	A	44.	C	74.	B	104.	A	134.	B
15.	A	45.	D	75.	B	105.	A	135.	A
16.	B	46.	A	76.	A	106.	B	136.	B
17.	B	47.	D	77.	B	107.	A	137.	C
18.	C	48.	A	78.	D	108.	B	138.	D
19.	C	49.	C	79.	C	109.	C	139.	B
20.	A	50.	D	80.	A	110.	D	140.	A
21.	D	51.	A	81.	A	111.	B	141.	C
22.	A	52.	B	82.	C	112.	D	142.	D
23.	C	53.	B	83.	B	113.	A	143.	A
24.	D	54.	B	84.	A	114.	B	144.	B
25.	D	55.	C	85.	B	115.	D	145.	D
26.	A	56.	A	86.	D	116.	B	146.	A
27.	A	57.	B	87.	C	117.	C	147.	B
28.	A	58.	A	88.	D	118.	C	148.	D
29.	B	59.	D	89.	C	119.	D	149.	A
30.	A	60.	C	90.	B	120.	C	150.	D

1. **C) Foreclosure**

This is the legal process where a lender seeks to recover the balance of a loan by selling the property held as collateral. Foreclosure usually occurs after a lender has legally obtained a termination of the borrower's right of redemption.

2.   **A) Asbestos**

Asbestos is a naturally occurring mineral and its insulation qualities make it popular in making fireproof materials. When products containing asbestos are disturbed, they release tiny fibers in the air that when inhaled over a long period of time can be detrimental as they accumulate in the lung causing scarring and inflammation. Continued exposure affects cells resulting in a rare cancer known as mesothelioma.

3.   **D) Studs**

These are vertical beams that are used during construction to frame the house. They are used to form or position walls in a building. Previously, studs made of timber dominated the construction industry but modern construction styles have embraced the use of steel.

4.   **A) Misrepresentation**

Misrepresentation occurs when a broker misstates information of property. It is a false statement that may affect a person's decision to enter into a contract. Three types of misrepresentation are fraudulent misrepresentation, negligent misrepresentation and innocent misrepresentation.

5   **C) Preventive maintenance**

In order to maintain tenants and an acceptable return on an investment, routine checks and repairs have to be done. These are done to safeguard against failing which may incur losses to the property manager that arise due to cost of replacement.

6.   **B) Mortgagee**

A mortgagee is an entity that lends money for the purpose of buying a real estate property. As a precaution, the mortgagee establishes prior interest in the property and maintains the title as collateral.

7.   **D) $156,250**

$150,000 / (1 - 0.04) = $156,250

8.   **C) Land zoning**

This refers to the restriction of physical development and the use of certain parcels of land. It is done with regard to zoning laws and purposes to protect wildlife and natural resources. It is also used to restrict the number of domestic animals that can be accommodated on a property.

9. **C) Initiate judicial foreclosure**

Judicial foreclosure are court proceedings that allow the lender to seize the property that was held as collateral for sale. This is done in order to regain the principal amount. This can only be done once it has been established that a defaulting borrower is unable to continue making payments

10. **B) CERCLA**

This is a trade association that is aimed at trying to improve oversight by representing title insurance. It considers a mortgage a high risk and therefore title insurance must be taken to protect lender

11. **C) Fair Credit Reporting Act**

Credit reporting is the process of collecting and analyzing consumers credit information by credit bureaus. This information is sold to lending facilities in order to help them determine whether or not a borrower is eligible for a loan. This act was passed to highlight consumer rights when it comes to credit information.

12. **C) Right of egress**

This is the legal right granted to homeowners as they allow access to property. These rights are usually obtained through an easement and apply regardless of the property type.

13. **A) Sweat equity**

This is the non-monetary equity that owners contribute into the business or property. In this case, sweat equity is the amount of effort an owner puts into a property in order to increase its value.

14. **A) Buydown**

This is a mortgage-financing technique that allows a borrower to negotiate lower monthly payment rates. It usually involves the seller making payments to the lending institution to reduce monthly payment rate of the buyer. As a result, the purchase price goes up.

15. **A) Clear title**

A clear title is a title that has no liens or levies from creditors and other involved parties. A clear title is used to ensure there is no question of ownership. It shows that there are no outstanding financial responsibilities attached to the property and the owner is legally capable of selling the property.

16. **B) Credit report**

A credit report is a detailed breakdown of an individual's credit history and is usually carried out by credit bureaus. They use financial information attached to an individual like their bill payment to establish a unique report. This information is usually used by lenders while considering a loan applicant.

17. **B) Equity**

Equity is another term for ownership. In home investments, equity means the amount of principal that has been paid off. The higher the equity the easier it is to refinance a property.

18. **C) Notice of default**

This is a public notice filed in court regarding a borrower's default on a loan. It is usually to notify the borrower that there has been a breach in the contractual limit that had been predetermined in the loan. A grace period is included for negotiation before further action is considered.

19. **C) Lock-in period**

This is the period usually 30 to 60 days within which a lender is required to keep a loan offer open. This gives the borrower enough time to prepare for closing while the lender is processing the loan. A lock in period protects the borrower from losses incurred throughout the repayment of the loan caused by rising interest rates during processing of the loan.

20. **A) When a tenant breaks a rent prior to the date of expiry without a legal reason**

As a lease is a contract, breaking a lease without a valid reason may result in being sued by the landlord. To avoid legal action, the individual breaking the lease must prove beyond reasonable doubt that the break was caused by a situation completely out of their hands.

21. **D) Shortfall**

Shortfall is a term used to describe a situation where a financial obligation exceeds the required amount of cash available. A shortfall may be a temporary and current situation or a prolonged one. The latter represents mismanagement of funds and warrants a deeper look into spending habits and change has to be implemented.

22. **A) Tax abatement**

Tax abatement is a strategy used by the government to increase investments in specific areas. In the real estate sector, tax abatement occurs when taxes on properties are significantly reduced or completely eliminated. It is usually done to encourage investors to buy property in areas that have recorded long term low demand.

23. **C) $546,000**

$500,000 * 1.04 * 1.05 = $546,000

24. **D) Department of Health**

25. **D) $368,000**

$92,000 / 0.25 = $368,000

26. **A) Abstract of title**

This is a summarized history of all title transfers and legal actions that have been connected with a certain property. It is beneficial in preventing home buyers from getting tangled in legal issues that are attached to a property. This is because any loss made because of a court ruling on a property once a buyer has purchased will be incurred by the new tenant.

27. **A) Flashing**

This is a material used to cover joints where two or more types of material join. This usually happens to prevent water leakage through the joint. It also provides a drainage between two joints.

28. **A) Eaves**

This is a part of the roof that projects over the wall beyond the edge of the roof. It is usually set in place to channel water away from the roof.

29. **B) Cash on cash return**

Cash on cash return that a proven metric used to calculate future cash returns on a cash investment. This metric is only true for a cash investment and does not take into account loan investments.

30. **A) Architectural Review Board**

The Architectural Review Board is given the responsibility of upholding the visual integrity of a town. It is responsible for reviewing all exterior designs of all residential and commercial structures in a town. All new structures and structures that are up for alteration are required to provide a blueprint of the exterior design for printing. They are also charged with ensuring commercial signs conform to the towns design.

31. **B) Gross lease**

   A gross lease is a lease where a flat rent fee is paid. It includes rent and other utility fees such as taxes and insurance. A landlord is obligated to calculate a rate based on history or research. A negotiation between the tenant and landlord can also be reached on the services the tenant wants to be included in the lease.

32. **A) House rules**

   These are rules that are given to tenants of a coop or condo on the beginning of the contract regarding behavior within the complex. They are put in place to ensure a comfortable living space for all occupants. Failure to adhere to the rules may result in eviction.

33. **B) Absorption rate**

   This is a ration of the number of properties that have been sold against the number of properties that are available for sale within a specified area.

34. **B) Acceleration clause**

   This is a provision in a mortgage that allows the lender the right to demand the immediate settlement on a mortgage under certain predetermined conditions such as a borrower defaulting on a loan.

35. **A) Easement appurtenant**

   Easement appurtenant is an agreement that is transferable with ownership rights of a property. When a property is transferred through sale or inheritance, all rights and privileges attached to the land are automatically transferred to the new owner.

36. **B) Homeowner's warranty insurance**

   Homeowner's warranty insurance insures the homeowner from the builder's faults for a specified warranty period

37. **B) Adverse possession**

   This is a legal principle that allows a person who has been living on a specific land for a long period of time to take possession of the land without permission of the owner. The individual does not have to have a title to the land to acquire it. The title holder is capable of claiming his land by choosing to eject the squatter.

38. **C) Encumbrance**

   This is a limitation against a real estate property. It restricts the owner from transferring ownership of the title. It also prevents an owner from depreciating the value of the property.

39.   **C) Joists**

These are horizontal structural members used to frame an open space. They are often used in transferring loads to the vertical members of the structure. When used in floors, they provide stiffness in the framing systems.

40.   **B) Conveyance**

A conveyance or sale deed is a legally binding contract that transfers all ownership rights from the seller to the buyer. It usually states the agreed-on price, the date of the transaction and the obligations of the parties involved.

41.   **B) Non-solicitation order**

This is an order issued to broker and agents to prevent them from soliciting listings in designated areas

42.   **A) Colleges**

Despite the fact that all property is assessed to determine its value, universities, schools, parks, government institutions, religious organizations, and hospitals are exempt from property taxes. Veterans are also eligible from partial exemption from taxes.

43.   **A) Accountability**

Commingling is a contract breach where a fiduciary mixed funds belonging to a client with his own making it impossible to separate them. The accountability clause requires a fiduciary to be able to maintain an accurate report of documents and funds that he/she has been entrusted.

44.   **C) Eminent domain**

This is the government's power to take private land for public use under certain circumstances. It is defined by the Taking Clause of the Fifth Amendment which prohibits the taking of private land without just compensation. It emphasizes that the government can only take land for public use and offer just compensation on the land.

45.   **D) Refuse modifications for handicapped tenants**

Refuse to allow tenants to make reasonable structural modifications to a unit at the tenant's expense to allow the handicapped tenant full enjoyment of the property (Fair Housing Act). In accordance with the Fair Housing Act which is against discrimination in housing, multifamily buildings are expected to ensure accessibility for people using wheelchairs

46.   **A) The Americans with Disabilities Act of 1990**

This act was enacted to ensure disabled people are not discriminated against and have equal rights regarding access to employment and commercial facilities.

47.   **D) Tenancy at will**

This is a tenancy that is not bound by a lease and does not have an expiry or duration of tenancy. A predetermined payment plan is adhered and a tenant is flexible to terminate the tenancy without legal proceedings. It is a beneficial plan for landlords and tenants that seek flexibility.

48.   **A) $2,041**

($350,000 * 0.07) / 12 = $2,041

49.   **C) Civil Rights Act Amendment of 1974**

The Civil Rights act amendment of 1974 banned discrimination based on sex and credit in a congress proceeding. Women being offered maternity leave on the assumption that they were unable to work was rendered illegal and sexist teaching methods were discredited.

50.   **D) Handicaps and familial status**

The act protects people with disabilities and families with children. Pregnant women were also protected from illegal discrimination.

51.   **A) $70,000**

$500,000 * 0.14 = $70,000

52.   **B) Assessor**

An assessor is a government official that is engaged to determine the value of a property. The information gathered by an assessor is used to calculate future property taxes. Assessors maintain annual assessments at a uniform percentage of market value.

53.   **B) Amortization**

This is the scheduling of monthly mortgage payments showing breakdown of payment. When paying a mortgage loan for a property, the initial payments are put towards paying off the interest and less is allocated to the principal amount. As a borrower makes more payments, more is allocated to the principal and less to the interest.

54. **B) Real estate tax**

This is an ad valorem tax on the value of a property. It is levied annually on real estate by the government authority.

55. **C) Leverage**

This refers to money that has been borrowed to finance an investment property. The leverage concept works best when rent and property values are on the rise. Monthly mortgage payments for the rental property become constant which results in a rise in profits

56. **A) Forced air system**

A forced air system refers to any HVAC system that makes use of air ducts and vents to release temperature-controlled air into the building. A forced air system released filtered and dehumidified cold air into buildings and runs at an affordable price. A central air system on the other hand uses vents in the forced air system to provide cool and conditioned air.

57. **B) One year**

An individual is required to wait for an entire year after which the agent is required to prove with evidence that he/she is capable of being trustworthy and upholding the law with regard to the real estate sector.

58. **A) Board of directors**

A co-op is an alternative method to traditional housing. A board of directors is elected by the shareholders to run the corporation. They are responsible for vetting and doing background checks on potential new shareholders in the corporation. They are also responsible for upholding the values and regulations of the co-op and terminating tenancy of individuals found to be acting contrary to the rules.

59. **D) Abstraction method**

This is a method of estimating the value of a piece of land that is based on the going price of similar parcels of land within the area.

60. **C) Grantor**

This is the party that transfers ownership of property to buyer through a legal document known as a deed. The grantor is required to sign the deed admitting the transfer of ownership before closing. The deed is then filed at the county jurisdiction for public record.

61. **D) Radon**

Radon is a radioactive cancer-causing gas that comes from the natural breakdown of uranium in soil. The gas penetrates its way into houses from cracks and holes in the foundation. Testing for radon gas is mandatory during purchasing of a home in order to fix the problem by lowering the amount of radon gas available to the acceptable amounts.

62. **B) Riparian rights**

These are rights that arise when an individual owns land near a moving watercourse. These rights include swimming and irrigation. The rights only attach when there's a water on one side of the land. An individual is allowed to benefit from the water body without contaminating or altering the flow of the waterbody.

63. **D) Regulation Z**

It requires lenders to make comprehensive disclosure statements to borrowers for consumer loans. It is aimed at protecting consumers from misleading lending practices. Lenders are required to disclose interest rates, finance charges, explain terms used and respond to all complaints launched by the borrower. This law was passed to ensure that borrowers make informed credit choices.

64. **C) Right of first refusal**

This is the right given to a specific party to purchase or lease a property before it is open to bidding by other potential buyers. The party being offered the privilege is not obligated to buy the property. In the event that the party is not interested in the property, it is opened up to the public.

65. **A) Economic obsolescence**

This is the decrease in the market value of a property due to external factors that cannot be controlled by the property owner i.e. building of an interstate highway close to a prime property. Its value immediately decreases due to the noise pollution.

66. **A) Special agent**

A special agent is an agent whose services are only employed for a specific task. Once the task is completed a special agent no longer has authority to represent the client.

67. **A) Appraisal**

An appraisal in a professional opinion value assessment of a property and is independent of the market values of similar properties based on the fact that all properties are unique and cannot be compared to each other.

68. **A) Mechanic's lien**

This is a security interest in title of property for the benefit of those who supplied materials and offered professional services on the construction and renovation of a property. A mechanic's lien can be taken on both real and personal properties.

69. **C) Sill plate**

This is a horizontal member of a wall where vertical members of the building are attached. It usually lies between the foundation and floor frame.

70. **A) Phone**

This is because salespeople are considered independent contractors and therefore are not eligible for company benefits.

71. **C) First substantial contact**

This refers to the earliest practicable opportunity during a conversation with the consumer. An agency disclosure is to be provided to disclose and explain the nature of the representation in a real estate transaction.

72. **B) Guiding families with children into an apartment building with other families with children and away from other buildings**

Steering is an unlawful practice that violates the federal fair housing provisions. It is a practice in which brokers influence the choice of a prospective buyer or tenant.

73. **A) 1% of loan**

A value point is a fee paid directly to the lender at closing in exchange for a reduced interest rate and can lower a borrower's monthly mortgage payment.

74. **B) Independent contractors**

Independent contractors are hired to perform a service but are not included in the employee catalogue. Their main goal is to complete the task and the employing broker has no control over the process of yielding results or financial expenses incurred.

75. **B) Accessory building**

This is a building that is built separately from the main structure in a property. It is usually put to use for a specific purpose such as a shed, workshop or garage.

76. **A) Fee simple estate**

This provides absolute ownership of the land and allows the owner to do whatever they choose to with the land. This is the highest form of ownership in real estate.

77. **B) Income that is earned by one spouse during the marriage**

Community property is defined as everything that a married couple owns together. This includes income and property acquired during the duration of the marriage.

78. **D) Real property**

A fixture is physically property that is permanently attached to real property (on it or under it), that cannot be moved. Examples include ponds, canals, buildings and roads.

79. **C) Mutual Agreement**

An agreement between a buyer and a seller. It is a binding contract between the two parties and includes any contingencies.

80. **A) A listing agreement with the seller has been executed**

A listing agreement is a contract between the homeowner and a selling agent. It is a legal agreement that gives the selling agent the right to sell the home.

81. **A) An agreement between the mortgage company and borrower that shows the terms of the loan**

This binding note states the terms of the loan and that the borrower promises to for the loan. It also provides evidence of the loan and both parties must sign the note to make it legally binding.

82. **C) Constructive eviction**

A constructive eviction is when a tenant must move out because the landlord fails to do something which renders the property uninhabitable. The tenant needs to give notice of the condition and allow a reasonable amount of time for the landlord to fix it. If this does not occur, the tenant can move out.

83. **B) 7 days**

If a seller's disclosure notice is not provided to the buyer, then they buyer has 7 days to cancel the contract.

84. **A) Prohibits discrimination in housing due to age**

The Federal Fair Housing Law prohibits discrimination due to race, color, national origin, religion, sex, familiar status and disability. This act prohibits discrimination when renting or buying a home, getting a mortgage, seeking housing assistance or engaging in other housing-related activities.

85. **B) Physical deterioration**

This is the most obvious form of depreciation and can occur when maintenance does not keep up with natural wear and tear. It causes a loss of value to the property. There are two types of physical deterioration functional obsolescence and external obsolescence.

86. **D) Parking spaces**

Appurtenances are real property that is immovable or fixed to the land. Parking spaces and water rights are considered an appurtenance.

87. **C) When two or more parties create and operate a real estate investment**

A syndicate is when investors pool their financial and intellectual resources to invest in real estate properties. These investments are bigger than a party would be able to afford individually.

88. **D) All of the above**

The right of disposition is also a bundle of rights. It is a set of legal privileges that affords a real estate buyer when the transfer of title occurs.

89. **C) Square footage**

Land has three characteristics, immobility, indestructibility and uniqueness. Some of the characteristics are immovable and can be changed, but location is an immobile characteristic.

90. **B) Trade fixtures**

Trade fixtures are removable personal property that is attached by the tenant to a leased land for the purpose of business i.e. display county. The trade fixture must be removable without damage to the property.

91. **A) Uniform Probate Code**

The Uniform Probate Code states that when a spouse dies the surviving spouse can take an elective share on the death of their spouse. It is an act that was drafted by the National Conference of Commissioners on Uniform State Laws.

92. **A) Fee simple absolute**

The fee simple absolute is the maximum possible right of ownership in real property. It is a form of freehold ownership and continues forever.

93. **B) Deed restrictions**

An encumbrance is a limitation or liability against real estate. A lien, deed restriction, easements, encroachments and licenses are all encumbrances. It restricts the owner's ability to transfer the property title.

94. **C) Doctrine of Appropriation**

The Doctrine of Appropriation says that water rights are determined by priority of beneficial use. The first person to use water or divert the water for beneficial purposes can acquire the individual rights to the water.

95. **B) Using a part of a neighbor's property to access the side of a road**

Prescriptive easement is when the right to use another's land is acquired through continued use without permission. There are three different types of easement: easement in gross, easement appurtenant and prescriptive easement. Regulations differ from state to state.

96. **A) Life estate**

A life estate lasts the duration of a person's life. It is also called a life tenancy. The estate in real property ends at the death and ownership of the property reverts back to the original owner.

97. **D) Real Estate Investment Trust**

This company owns and operates income-producing real estate. REIT owns commercial property such as apartment buildings, warehouses, hospitals and shopping centers.

98. **A) Ad valorem tax**

The ad valorem tax is based on the value of the property. It is imposed at the time of a transaction just like a value-added tax.

99. **B) Monument**

A natural or manmade, fixed object that is used as a reference point for surveying land. It is a tangible landmark that has been established to indicate a boundary.

100. **A) A history of ownership regarding a property's title**

A chain of title goes back to the original owner of the property and is the sequence of historical transfers of title. A chain of title search typically goes back 40 years to ensure there are no defects.

101. **D) History**

There are five tests to determine what a fixture is. The five tests are method of attachment, adaptability, relationship of the parties, intention of the party, and agreement between the parties.

102. **C) Avulsion**

Avulsion occurs when there is a sudden loss of land due to water. It is the opposite of accretion which is an addition to land due to water.

103. **B) Severance**

Severance is the process of converting real property to personal property. There are two types of severance, actual and constructive.

104. **A) Cooperative**

A cooperative, or co-op, is when a buyer buys shares in a corporation that owns an apartment building. In exchange for buying the shares, the buyer receives the right to live in a specific unit.

105. **A) A buyer buys a house that has a condition in place stating that the original architecture features are never removed from the property**

A fee simple defeasible estate is a conveyance of property that has conditions in place. The property will revert back to the original grantor or a specified third party if the conditions are violated.

106. **B) Involuntary lien**

An involuntary lien is how the government pursues property owners who have not paid certain debts. In order for the property owner to get the lien removed, they must pay the taxes, interests and other fees.

107. **A) Voluntary tenancy**

Voluntary tenancy is not a distinct form of ownership in the state of California. The 6 forms are severalty, tenancy in common, joint tenancy, tenancy in partnership, community property and community property with the right of survivorship.

108. **B) Double step-up in basis**

The surviving spouse's tax basis in property is the total fair market value of the property when the deceased spouse died.

109. **C) Marketable title**

A marketable title is a title that the court of equity considers free from defect or liens and can be easily sold on the market.

110. **D) Allodial system**

This is the legal right of ownership of many legal systems in the United States and throughout the world.

111. **B) Mello-Roos**

This is a type of financing that is used in cities, counties and special districts (i.e. school districts). It is a type of parcel tax that circumvents proposition 13 which limits property taxes based on the assessed value of the real property.

112. **D) All of the above**

All of the above are true about disclosures to the buyer by the seller. The disclosure must be in writing, and it can affect the buyers desire to purchase or the amount they are willing to pay.

113. **A) Transfer Disclosure Statement**

This form is also called a TDS. The point of the document is to accurately describe the condition of the property.

114. **B) Multiple listing service**

This portal provides firms with an unlimited inventory of homes for sale. Only agents and professional affiliates have access to MLS.

115. **D) All of the above**

The laws of agency are a part of commercial law that deals with contractual fiduciary relationships that involve an agent who is authorized to act on behalf of the principal.

116.   **B) Supplemental Statutory Disclosure**

This form is used to cover several types of disclosures that are required by law but do not have their own disclosure form. The seller is required to fill out this form. Release of illegal controlled substance on the property is another example of what would need to be disclosed.

117.   **C) If property is transferred between spouses**

A transfer disclosure is needed for all sales except when the property is transferred between spouses.

118.   **C) It enhances the value of the property**

Full disclosure is helpful in the sale of property, is strengthens the trust between an agent and a principal and enhances the value of the property.

119.   **D) Seller agency**

This is the most common type of agency and is the relationship between an agent and seller. A contract is entered into between the agent and seller giving the agent the right to work on behalf of the seller.

120.   **C) Disclose, elect, confirm**

The agent must provide a disclosure form to the seller, buyer or both. The agent then must elect a legally permitted agency relationship and then the seller and buyer must confirm or agree to the agency relationship (in writing).

121.   **B) 3 years**

The supplemental statutory disclosure form is used to disclose a death within three years.

122.   **A) Within 48 hours**

A listing agreement needs to be submitted to MLS within 48 hours of signing the agreement, unless it was exempted.

123.   **C) Safety clause**

A safety clause is a protection in real estate deals that entitles a broker to a commission even after the listing expires or the listing is cancelled.

124.   **B) Listing agreements can be submitted to multiple MLS's**

There is no limit to how many multiple listing services a broker can list their principal's home. It can be submitted to multiple.

125. **A) Open listing**

Open listings and exclusive agency listings allow an owner to sell their home on their own and avoid paying commission.

126. **B) If the broker's license is invalid**

A listing agreement can be terminated if the license is invalid, if the seller or broker dies or if both the broker and seller agree to terminating the agreement.

127. **D) All of the above**

The Sherman act prohibits group boycotting, price fixing and market allocation. It is the first major legislation to address oppressive business practices.

128. **C) Unruh Act**

This California legislation outlaws discrimination by all business establishments in California, this includes housing and public accommodations.

129. **B) Allows only brokers to receive commissions**

The Real Estate Law states that only brokers can receive commissions in the state of California.

130. **A) When licensees encourage homeowners to sell due to an influx of minorities**

Blockbusting causes a decline of housing prices in the neighborhood and is illegal in all states. It was used to profit from prejudice driven market instability.

131. **B) A person cannot act as a foreclosure consultant without obtaining a Certificate of Registration**

California requires those who want to be a foreclosure consultant to be registered as a Mortgage of Foreclosure Consultant with the Department of Justice.

132. **C) Advertisement designed to attract disabled people to property modified for their needs**

California allows advertisements as the above, but setting restrictive standards of specific tenants or advertising based on race or religion does not comply with anti-discrimination laws.

133. **C) Market allocation**

Market allocation is when competitors agree to divide markets amongst themselves. Firms allocate specific customers among themselves.

134. **B) Rumford Fair Housing Act**

This act was passed in 1963 and helped to end racial discrimination by property owners and landlords, specifically those who refused to rent or sell property on the basis of race.

135. **A) Senior citizen housing**

The Unruh Act exempts discrimination when it comes to senior housing that has been designed to meet the physical and social needs of senior citizens. This type of housing can legally exclude households with children.

136. **B) Tie-in arrangement**

This type of agreement is illegal in the United States. It is when a party agrees to sell on the condition that the buyer also purchases another product.

137. **C) Do Not Call Registry**

Real estate agents must comply with the Do Not Call registry. Agents cannot call people on the registry to entice them to sell their properties or buy their home.

138. **D) Farming**

This is a type of marketing strategy that can grow into future business. It is typically done in an area close to the brokers business and involves planting, nurturing and cultivating leads.

139. **B) An opt-out option**

Prospecting in real estate requires an opt-out option, a working email address to reply to and the objective of the message in the subject line.

140. **A) Listing package**

A listing package is sent out to potential clients after they've scheduled an appointment for a listing presentation. A good packet will include a property profile, sample flyers and brochures and the establishment of trust and communication.

141. **C) Overpricing**

Overpricing a home can cause the property to fail to sell. It could end also up costing the seller more in the long run.

142. **D) Pocket listing**

This occurs when a broker holds a signed listing agreement with a seller by never advertising. Pocket listings are legal if they are done in the best interest of the client.

143. **A) County tax assessor's office**

The tax assessor's office has property cards that have the owner's name, legal address and other information such as annual property taxes.

144. **B) Shows how land is divided into lots in each county**

The maps are drawn to scale, and the records show the land's size, boundary locations, streets, flood zones and easements or rights of way.

145. **D) California Business and Professions Code 17500**

This code prohibits false advertisement which can have adverse actions such as civil penalties.

146. **A) Contingent offer**

This type of offer is dependent upon meeting certain criteria. If the criteria are met, the deal will advance to a pending state.

147. **B) If the buyer and seller agree to cancel the deal**

A full refund of a good faith deposit can be refunded if both the buyer and the seller agree to cancel the deal without incurring any third-party costs that may require a reimbursement.

148. **D) 21 days**

A buyer has 21 days to complete property inspections, investigations, obtain financing and determine if they would like to move forward with the deal.

149. **A) 3**

Earnest money needs to be deposited within 3 days of receiving it by the broker. Earnest money is typically between 1-3 percent of the purchase price.

150. **D) A&B only**

The seller and the buyer both have the ability to modify an accepted offer. The broker does not. To modify the offer, a written consent needs to be provided by the buyer and seller.

Practice Test 3

Directions:

1.   You have 3 hours to complete the exam.

2.   To pass, you must answer at least 105 out of 150 questions correctly.

3.   Some questions will require mathematics. You may use a calculator.

4.   **Phones and pagers are not allowed. Having either will result in automatic dismissal from the exam and nullification of exam scores.**

Tips:

- Answer all questions even if you are unsure.
- Mark any questions you are stuck on and revisit them after you are done. The exam is timed so make sure you finish as many questions as you can.
- After reading the question, try answering it in your head first to avoid getting confused by the choices.
- Read the entire question before looking at the answers.
- Use the process of elimination to filter out choices that don't seem correct to increase your chances of selecting the correct answer.
- Be aware of important keywords like **not, sometimes, always,** and **never**. These words completely alter the ask of the question so it's important to keep track of them.

PLEASE READ THESE INSTRUCTIONS CAREFULLY.

Practice Test 3

Name: _____   Date: _____

1. Ⓐ Ⓑ Ⓒ Ⓓ	31. Ⓐ Ⓑ Ⓒ Ⓓ	61. Ⓐ Ⓑ Ⓒ Ⓓ
2. Ⓐ Ⓑ Ⓒ Ⓓ	32. Ⓐ Ⓑ Ⓒ Ⓓ	62. Ⓐ Ⓑ Ⓒ Ⓓ
3. Ⓐ Ⓑ Ⓒ Ⓓ	33. Ⓐ Ⓑ Ⓒ Ⓓ	63. Ⓐ Ⓑ Ⓒ Ⓓ
4. Ⓐ Ⓑ Ⓒ Ⓓ	34. Ⓐ Ⓑ Ⓒ Ⓓ	64. Ⓐ Ⓑ Ⓒ Ⓓ
5. Ⓐ Ⓑ Ⓒ Ⓓ	35. Ⓐ Ⓑ Ⓒ Ⓓ	65. Ⓐ Ⓑ Ⓒ Ⓓ
6. Ⓐ Ⓑ Ⓒ Ⓓ	36. Ⓐ Ⓑ Ⓒ Ⓓ	66. Ⓐ Ⓑ Ⓒ Ⓓ
7. Ⓐ Ⓑ Ⓒ Ⓓ	37. Ⓐ Ⓑ Ⓒ Ⓓ	67. Ⓐ Ⓑ Ⓒ Ⓓ
8. Ⓐ Ⓑ Ⓒ Ⓓ	38. Ⓐ Ⓑ Ⓒ Ⓓ	68. Ⓐ Ⓑ Ⓒ Ⓓ
9. Ⓐ Ⓑ Ⓒ Ⓓ	39. Ⓐ Ⓑ Ⓒ Ⓓ	69. Ⓐ Ⓑ Ⓒ Ⓓ
10. Ⓐ Ⓑ Ⓒ Ⓓ	40. Ⓐ Ⓑ Ⓒ Ⓓ	70. Ⓐ Ⓑ Ⓒ Ⓓ
11. Ⓐ Ⓑ Ⓒ Ⓓ	41. Ⓐ Ⓑ Ⓒ Ⓓ	71. Ⓐ Ⓑ Ⓒ Ⓓ
12. Ⓐ Ⓑ Ⓒ Ⓓ	42. Ⓐ Ⓑ Ⓒ Ⓓ	72. Ⓐ Ⓑ Ⓒ Ⓓ
13. Ⓐ Ⓑ Ⓒ Ⓓ	43. Ⓐ Ⓑ Ⓒ Ⓓ	73. Ⓐ Ⓑ Ⓒ Ⓓ
14. Ⓐ Ⓑ Ⓒ Ⓓ	44. Ⓐ Ⓑ Ⓒ Ⓓ	74. Ⓐ Ⓑ Ⓒ Ⓓ
15. Ⓐ Ⓑ Ⓒ Ⓓ	45. Ⓐ Ⓑ Ⓒ Ⓓ	75. Ⓐ Ⓑ Ⓒ Ⓓ
16. Ⓐ Ⓑ Ⓒ Ⓓ	46. Ⓐ Ⓑ Ⓒ Ⓓ	76. Ⓐ Ⓑ Ⓒ Ⓓ
17 Ⓐ Ⓑ Ⓒ Ⓓ	47. Ⓐ Ⓑ Ⓒ Ⓓ	77. Ⓐ Ⓑ Ⓒ Ⓓ
18. Ⓐ Ⓑ Ⓒ Ⓓ	48. Ⓐ Ⓑ Ⓒ Ⓓ	78. Ⓐ Ⓑ Ⓒ Ⓓ
19. Ⓐ Ⓑ Ⓒ Ⓓ	49. Ⓐ Ⓑ Ⓒ Ⓓ	79. Ⓐ Ⓑ Ⓒ Ⓓ
20. Ⓐ Ⓑ Ⓒ Ⓓ	50. Ⓐ Ⓑ Ⓒ Ⓓ	80. Ⓐ Ⓑ Ⓒ Ⓓ
21. Ⓐ Ⓑ Ⓒ Ⓓ	51. Ⓐ Ⓑ Ⓒ Ⓓ	81. Ⓐ Ⓑ Ⓒ Ⓓ
22. Ⓐ Ⓑ Ⓒ Ⓓ	52. Ⓐ Ⓑ Ⓒ Ⓓ	82. Ⓐ Ⓑ Ⓒ Ⓓ
23. Ⓐ Ⓑ Ⓒ Ⓓ	53. Ⓐ Ⓑ Ⓒ Ⓓ	83. Ⓐ Ⓑ Ⓒ Ⓓ
24. Ⓐ Ⓑ Ⓒ Ⓓ	54. Ⓐ Ⓑ Ⓒ Ⓓ	84. Ⓐ Ⓑ Ⓒ Ⓓ
25. Ⓐ Ⓑ Ⓒ Ⓓ	55. Ⓐ Ⓑ Ⓒ Ⓓ	85. Ⓐ Ⓑ Ⓒ Ⓓ
26. Ⓐ Ⓑ Ⓒ Ⓓ	56. Ⓐ Ⓑ Ⓒ Ⓓ	86. Ⓐ Ⓑ Ⓒ Ⓓ
27. Ⓐ Ⓑ Ⓒ Ⓓ	57. Ⓐ Ⓑ Ⓒ Ⓓ	87. Ⓐ Ⓑ Ⓒ Ⓓ
28. Ⓐ Ⓑ Ⓒ Ⓓ	58. Ⓐ Ⓑ Ⓒ Ⓓ	88. Ⓐ Ⓑ Ⓒ Ⓓ
29. Ⓐ Ⓑ Ⓒ Ⓓ	59. Ⓐ Ⓑ Ⓒ Ⓓ	89. Ⓐ Ⓑ Ⓒ Ⓓ
30. Ⓐ Ⓑ Ⓒ Ⓓ	60. Ⓐ Ⓑ Ⓒ Ⓓ	90. Ⓐ Ⓑ Ⓒ Ⓓ

Practice Test 3

Name: _____   Date: _____

91.	Ⓐ	Ⓑ	Ⓒ	Ⓓ	121.	Ⓐ	Ⓑ	Ⓒ	Ⓓ
92.	Ⓐ	Ⓑ	Ⓒ	Ⓓ	122.	Ⓐ	Ⓑ	Ⓒ	Ⓓ
93.	Ⓐ	Ⓑ	Ⓒ	Ⓓ	123.	Ⓐ	Ⓑ	Ⓒ	Ⓓ
94.	Ⓐ	Ⓑ	Ⓒ	Ⓓ	124.	Ⓐ	Ⓑ	Ⓒ	Ⓓ
95.	Ⓐ	Ⓑ	Ⓒ	Ⓓ	125.	Ⓐ	Ⓑ	Ⓒ	Ⓓ
96.	Ⓐ	Ⓑ	Ⓒ	Ⓓ	126.	Ⓐ	Ⓑ	Ⓒ	Ⓓ
97.	Ⓐ	Ⓑ	Ⓒ	Ⓓ	127.	Ⓐ	Ⓑ	Ⓒ	Ⓓ
98.	Ⓐ	Ⓑ	Ⓒ	Ⓓ	128.	Ⓐ	Ⓑ	Ⓒ	Ⓓ
99.	Ⓐ	Ⓑ	Ⓒ	Ⓓ	129.	Ⓐ	Ⓑ	Ⓒ	Ⓓ
100.	Ⓐ	Ⓑ	Ⓒ	Ⓓ	130.	Ⓐ	Ⓑ	Ⓒ	Ⓓ
101.	Ⓐ	Ⓑ	Ⓒ	Ⓓ	131.	Ⓐ	Ⓑ	Ⓒ	Ⓓ
102.	Ⓐ	Ⓑ	Ⓒ	Ⓓ	132.	Ⓐ	Ⓑ	Ⓒ	Ⓓ
103.	Ⓐ	Ⓑ	Ⓒ	Ⓓ	133.	Ⓐ	Ⓑ	Ⓒ	Ⓓ
104.	Ⓐ	Ⓑ	Ⓒ	Ⓓ	134.	Ⓐ	Ⓑ	Ⓒ	Ⓓ
105.	Ⓐ	Ⓑ	Ⓒ	Ⓓ	135.	Ⓐ	Ⓑ	Ⓒ	Ⓓ
106.	Ⓐ	Ⓑ	Ⓒ	Ⓓ	136.	Ⓐ	Ⓑ	Ⓒ	Ⓓ
107	Ⓐ	Ⓑ	Ⓒ	Ⓓ	137.	Ⓐ	Ⓑ	Ⓒ	Ⓓ
108.	Ⓐ	Ⓑ	Ⓒ	Ⓓ	138.	Ⓐ	Ⓑ	Ⓒ	Ⓓ
109.	Ⓐ	Ⓑ	Ⓒ	Ⓓ	139.	Ⓐ	Ⓑ	Ⓒ	Ⓓ
110.	Ⓐ	Ⓑ	Ⓒ	Ⓓ	140.	Ⓐ	Ⓑ	Ⓒ	Ⓓ
111.	Ⓐ	Ⓑ	Ⓒ	Ⓓ	141.	Ⓐ	Ⓑ	Ⓒ	Ⓓ
112.	Ⓐ	Ⓑ	Ⓒ	Ⓓ	142.	Ⓐ	Ⓑ	Ⓒ	Ⓓ
113.	Ⓐ	Ⓑ	Ⓒ	Ⓓ	143.	Ⓐ	Ⓑ	Ⓒ	Ⓓ
114.	Ⓐ	Ⓑ	Ⓒ	Ⓓ	144.	Ⓐ	Ⓑ	Ⓒ	Ⓓ
115.	Ⓐ	Ⓑ	Ⓒ	Ⓓ	145.	Ⓐ	Ⓑ	Ⓒ	Ⓓ
116.	Ⓐ	Ⓑ	Ⓒ	Ⓓ	146.	Ⓐ	Ⓑ	Ⓒ	Ⓓ
117.	Ⓐ	Ⓑ	Ⓒ	Ⓓ	147.	Ⓐ	Ⓑ	Ⓒ	Ⓓ
118.	Ⓐ	Ⓑ	Ⓒ	Ⓓ	148.	Ⓐ	Ⓑ	Ⓒ	Ⓓ
119.	Ⓐ	Ⓑ	Ⓒ	Ⓓ	149.	Ⓐ	Ⓑ	Ⓒ	Ⓓ
120.	Ⓐ	Ⓑ	Ⓒ	Ⓓ	150.	Ⓐ	Ⓑ	Ⓒ	Ⓓ

1. What is the name given to the estimate amount on a mortgage?

   A. Pre-approval
   B. Post-approval
   C. Principal
   D. Mortgage

2. What is the actual amount of space a tenant can lay carpet and place furniture?

   A. Usable Square Footage
   B. Rentable square footage
   C. Common areas
   D. Service areas

3. What is the name given to an amount of money borrowed to facilitate the purchase of a property?

   A. Escrow
   B. Interest
   C. Down payment
   D. Principal

4. What type of mortgage loan is made available through the United States Department of Veterans Affairs?

   A. Blanket mortgage
   B. Balloon mortgage
   C. Graduated mortgage
   D. VA mortgage

5. What is the value obtained by deducting applied payments from original amortization?

   A. Full term
   B. Paid term
   C. Principal term
   D. Remaining term

6. What is the arrangement that allows a seller to lease a property from a purchaser after selling it?

   A. Leaseback
   B. Leasehold
   C. Sublease
   D. Proprietary lease

7. What type of easement attaches rights to a tenant instead of the land?

   A. Easement appurtenant
   B. Easement in gross
   C. Prescriptive easement
   D. All the above

8. What is the penalty charge for paying back a loan ahead of the scheduled payment plan?

   A. Defaulting penalty
   B. Interest
   C. Prepayment penalty
   D. Principal amount

9. What is an insurance premium paid by the buyer to the lender in order to protect the lender from default on a mortgage?

    A. Hazard insurance
    B. Homeowner's insurance
    C. Private mortgage insurance
    D. Title insurance

10. What is the name given to a party that acts in conjunction with a lender to originate a loan?

    A. Mortgage broker
    B. Third party originator
    C. Lender
    D. Intermediate

11. What is the term used to describe the alteration of a property in order to increase its market value?

    A. Capital Improvement
    B. Preventive maintenance
    C. Appreciation
    D. Common charges

12. What is the tax levied on transfer of property?

    A. Capital gains tax
    B. Deductible tax
    C. Property tax
    D. Transfer tax

13. Which of the following is an appraisal method in real estate?

    A. Sales Comparison Approach
    B. Cost Approach
    C. Income Approach
    D. All of the above

14. For at least how long must an asset be held before being sold to be categorized as long-term capital gains?

    A. One month
    B. Six months
    C. One year
    D. Two years

15. Which of these is considered an operating expense?

    A. Repairs
    B. Depreciation
    C. Payroll
    D. All of the above

16. What is an unlawful detainer?

    A. Forcing rent payments for tenants who have already moved out
    B. Refusing to leave a property despite expiration or termination of lease
    C. Listing a property whose lease has not expired
    D. Subletting a property without permission from the landlord

17. What is the freeze placed on a mortgage loan for a period of time?

   A. Cessation
   B. Amortization
   C. Rate lock
   D. Interest freeze

18. What type of lease gives the tenant an option to purchase the property?

   A. Leaseback
   B. Lease option
   C. Leasehold
   D. Gross lease

19. What is conditioner capacity?

   A. This is the capacity of an air conditioner to heat or cool the room
   B. The space used up by an air conditioner
   C. The strength of an air conditioner
   D. The cooling capacity of an air conditioner and is measured in tons

20. What is the name given to an individual that acts in intermediate for brokers and lenders?

   A. Mortgage broker
   B. Mortgage banker
   C. Attorney
   D. Intermediate

21. If a property is taxed at 30% with a tax levy of $105,000, what is its assessed value?

   A. $136,500
   B. $146,666
   C. $350,000
   D. None of the above

22. What is the notice given when a tenant has a pet in a complex that has no pets policy?

   A. Notice to cure
   B. Notice to quit
   C. Notice of default
   D. Notice of termination

23. What is a roof's vertical rise in inches divided by its horizontal span in feet?

   A. Depth
   B. Width
   C. Pitch
   D. Length

24. Who engages the services of a broker?

   A. The client
   B. The neighbor
   C. The contractor
   D. The appraiser

25. Right of way would be best defined as?

    A. Escheat
    B. Easement
    C. Right of ingress
    D. Encumbrance

26. Who can get partial exemptions from property taxes?

    A. Disabled
    B. Schools
    C. Shelters
    D. Markets

27. What age must a person be to get a Real Estate license?

    A. 16 years
    B. 18 years
    C. 30 years
    D. 43 years

28. Which electricity conductor plays the same role as a circuit board?

    A. Cell
    B. Capacitor
    C. Fuse
    D. Switch

29. What is the definition of a bilateral contract?

    A. A contract that involves only the promisor
    B. A contract that involves only the promisee
    C. A contract that involves both a promisor and promisee
    D. A contract that allows both parties to drop all claims and get out of the contract

30. What is real property tax based on?

    A. Assessed value
    B. CMA
    C. Appraisal
    D. Taxable value

31. What agency is responsible for protecting wetlands?

    A. CERCLA
    B. Environmental Protection Agency
    C. FEMA
    D. NY Health Department

32. What is a schedule of the projected future income and expenses for a real estate investment?

    A. IOU
    B. Invoice
    C. Promissory note
    D. Pro Forma Statement

33. What is an agent required to do if a client refuses to sign an agency disclosure form?

   A. Terminate relationship
   B. Create record of refusal in writing
   C. Continue without record of the refusal
   D. Take legal action against the client

34. What is a general voluntary lien?

   A. Mortgage
   B. Taxes
   C. Revenues
   D. Duties

35. If a salesperson's commission is not paid, he resorts to?

   A. Buyer
   B. Seller
   C. Broker
   D. Lender

36. What type of tenancy exists where property is owned by a single individual?

   A. Joint tenancy
   B. Ownership in severalty
   C. Tenancy in entirety
   D. Tenancy in common

37. Who are testers in real estate?

   A. People who pose as real estate clients to check if fair housing is being practiced
   B. People who assess the value of a property
   C. People who pose as borrowers to ensure proper loaning practices
   D. People who approach the seller without the intention of buying

38. What is the term used to describe the natural increase of land?

   A. Expansion
   B. Avulsion
   C. Erosion
   D. Accretion

39. What is the length of time allowed for depreciation for a residential property?

   A. 5 years
   B. 27.5 years
   C. 39 years
   D. 70 years

40. What is the term used to describe personal property?

   A. Chattel
   B. Investment
   C. Possession
   D. Real property

41. Which act was enacted to ensure parties involved in a real estate transaction receive complete settlement cost disclosure?

    A.   RESPA
    B.   FHA
    C.   Clean Water Act
    D.   Civil Rights Act

42. What is the name given to the downward movement of water through soil?

    A.   Absorption
    B.   Filtration
    C.   Percolation
    D.   Proration

43. What type of income is generated by investing in a limited partnership?

    A.   Active income
    B.   Passive income
    C.   Surplus income
    D.   Savings

44. What mortgage type allows the mortgagor to make payments only on the interest accrued?

    A.   Blanket mortgage
    B.   Balloon mortgage
    C.   Graduated mortgage
    D.   Straight term mortgage

45. Mary's agent helped her purchase a property and negotiated a mortgage for her. This agent also represented the seller. What type of agent did Mary engage?

    A.   Single agent
    B.   Dual agent
    C.   Double agent
    D.   None of the above

46. What is the land survey process that involves the surveyor starting at an easily identifiable point and describing the property in terms of courses and distances and eventually returning to the starting point?

    A.   ALTA
    B.   Boundary construction
    C.   Metes and bounds
    D.   Topographic surveys

47. What arrangement allows the seller to absorb an existing loan in order to allow the buyer another mortgage?

    A.   Simple mortgage
    B.   Wraparound mortgage
    C.   Mortgage by conditional sale
    D.   Reverse mortgage

48. Which real estate participants are legally required to be licensed?

    A.   Sellers
    B.   Buyers
    C.   Lenders
    D.   Real estate agents and brokers

49. What is the term used to refer to the act of mixing money belonging to a client with one's own funds?

    A. Commingling
    B. Investing
    C. Stealing
    D. Saving

50. What is the effect of a larger money supply on the interest rates?

    A. They decrease
    B. They increase
    C. Remains constant
    D. They have no relationship

51. What is a homeowner's policy that covers two parts: property and liability?

    A. HO1
    B. HO2
    C. HO3
    D. HO4

52. What is the name given to tax calculated based on the value of an asset?

    A. Ad valorem tax
    B. Property tax
    C. Capital gains tax
    D. Transfer tax

53. What kind of lease agreement requires the landlord to pay for all expenses?

    A. Gross lease
    B. Ground lease
    C. Net lease
    D. Sublease

54. If a seller nets $442,000 from the sale of her home, and the commission is 5%, how much did the home sell for?

    A. $464,100
    B. $420,952
    C. $459,680
    D. None of the above

55. What is the short-term loan that covers the interval between selling one property and buying another?

    A. Bridge Loan
    B. Cash flow
    C. Cash on cash return
    D. Mortgage

56. What are the set rules established for condominium or co-op tenants?

    A. House rules
    B. Investment agreement
    C. Regulations
    D. Policy

57. Who is responsible for the rent in a sublease?

    A. New tenant
    B. Lessee
    C. Lessor
    D. Roommate

58. What income type does a salary fall under?

    A. Active income
    B. Passive income
    C. Savings
    D. Investment

59. What is the name given to an estate that gives the holder temporary possession rights?

    A. Concurrent estates
    B. Estate for years
    C. Freehold estates
    D. Leasehold estate

60. What is a permit issued to a builder stating the property is fit for occupancy?

    A. Certificate of occupancy
    B. Contract of sale
    C. Landmark designation
    D. Receipt of sales deposit

61. What kind of mortgage pays off the principal?

    A. Amortized loan
    B. Fixed- rate loan
    C. Floating rate loan
    D. Mortgage

62. What is the income that is left after all operating costs are paid in a real estate investment?

    A. Investment
    B. Net operating income
    C. Profit
    D. Revenue

63. Which lease allows for changes in rent within the lease term?

    A. Graduated lease
    B. Lease break
    C. Sublease
    D. Value point

64. What is the married couple's capital gains tax exclusion on the sale of their primary home?

    A. $50,000
    B. $75,000
    C. $250,000
    D. $500,000

65. What should a licensee do with their pocket card?

   A. Advertise it
   B. Carry a physical copy or have a digital image on a device
   C. File it
   D. Use it to get clients

66. Besides the real estate agents, who is eligible for a license?

   A. Attorney
   B. Broker
   C. Mortgage broker
   D. Lender

67. What is a single person's capital gains tax exclusion?

   A. $25,000
   B. $100,000
   C. $250,000
   D. $500,000

68. What is the term given to violation of neighbor's property by trespassing?

   A. Easement
   B. Escheat
   C. Encroachment
   D. Encumbrance

69. What type of insurance is referred to as renter's insurance?

   A. HO1
   B. HO2
   C. HO3
   D. HO4

70. What is a form of co-ownership by which all parties have undivided interests in the property but no right of survivorship?

   A. Tenancy in common
   B. Tenancy in entirety
   C. Joint tenancy
   D. Ownership in severalty

71. What conveys a grantor's interest in real property?

   A. Deed
   B. Insurance
   C. Title
   D. Warrant

72. What is the chain of deeds and other documents used in transferring title of land from one owner to another consecutively?

   A. Abstract of title
   B. Deed chain
   C. History of deed
   D. Chain of title

73. If you paid a down payment of $200,000 for a property worth $1,000,000 dollars and you currently rent it out for $4,000 a month, what is the cash on cash return?

    A.   4%
    B.   4.8%
    C.   20%
    D.   24%

74. What is a Certificate of Eligibility?

    A.   Certificate that shows one is to be exempt from property tax
    B.   Certificate that is presented by veterans to show proof that they have met the minimum service requirements to be eligible for a VA loan
    C.   Certificate that shows a construction is fit for occupancy
    D.   Certificate that shows merit

75. What is the insurance policy that protects a lender from loss due to disputes over ownership of a property and defects in the title?

    A.   Hazard insurance
    B.   Home warranty
    C.   Homeowner's insurance
    D.   Title insurance

76. Property that has a divided form of ownership is called?

    A.   Cooperative
    B.   Planned unit development
    C.   Time-share
    D.   Joint tenants

77. What is the definition of a syndication?

    A.   Income that is earned by a spouse prior to marriage
    B.   Land that is divided into smaller pieces of land
    C.   Mutual funds that invest in rental properties
    D.   Real estate that is purchased by a group which includes at least one sponsor and several investors

78. Which of the following is **not** an essential element of a contract?

    A.   Notarized signature
    B.   Consideration
    C.   Agreement by offer and acceptance
    D.   Competent parties

79. Which listing agreement allows the owner of the listed property to sell the property on their own and not have to pay commission to the listing broker?

    A.   Open listing
    B.   Option listing
    C.   Exclusive agency listing
    D.   Both A and C

80. What is the listing agreement that gives the broker the payment of commission no matter who sells the property?

    A.   Entirety
    B.   Exclusive-right-to-sell listing
    C.   Open listing
    D.   Net Listing

81. Which is an example of functional obsolescence?

    A. Four bedrooms and one bathroom in a private residence
    B. All bedrooms located on the 2nd floor and only one bathroom located on the 1st floor
    C. Walking through one bedroom to get to another bedroom
    D. All of the above

82. Which act was passed to protect consumers from being scammed when purchasing raw land?

    A. Interstate Land Sales Full Disclosure Act
    B. Federal Fair Housing Act
    C. Equal Credit Opportunity Act
    D. Federal Real Estate Law

83. Which statement is a listing agent required to reveal to a prospective buyer?

    A. The physical health of the previous owner
    B. Renovations made within the last 5 years
    C. Re-zoning of a property
    D. The number of members living in a home

84. Real estate taxes are based on the value of a home. A property owner can be taxed additionally to help pay for projects that benefit the neighborhood. What is this type of tax called?

    A. Property tax
    B. Special assessment tax
    C. Progressive tax
    D. Capital gains tax

85. Which anti-trust violation applies to real estate?

    A. Monopolization
    B. Price-fixing
    C. Collusion
    D. None of the above

86. A _____ transfers a title of real property without the owner's consent.

    A. Involuntary alienation
    B. Redlining
    C. Lien
    D. Deed restriction

87. Which of the following is a common-law fiduciary duty?

    A. Care
    B. Accounting
    C. Confidentiality
    D. All of the above

88. Which type of lease increases at specific intervals?

    A. Lease option
    B. Graduated lease
    C. Month to month lease
    D. Triple net lease

89. A _____ can be granted by a zoning board if a property owner demonstrates a need to deviate from the current zoning requirements.

    A. Variance
    B. Moratorium
    C. Quitclaim
    D. Encumbrance

90. A defect that is not apparent after an ordinary inspection is called a(n) _____.

    A. Undisclosed defect
    B. Material defect
    C. Arbitration
    D. Latent defect

91. Which of the following statement(s) is(are) true about an option to purchase agreement?

    A. The seller is required to accept any offer that meets all of their needs
    B. The buyer is required to buy the property once the option agreement has been completed
    C. The seller can change their mind about the offer if a better offer has been received
    D. All of the above

92. Which type of loan requires the debt ratio to not exceed 41%?

    A. Federal Housing Administration loan
    B. VA loan
    C. Interest-only mortgage
    D. Adjustable rate mortgage

93. What is the difference between a lien theory and a title theory?

    A. Lien theory is when the title is held by the lender until the final payment is made

    B. Title theory is when the title is held by the borrower

    C. Lien theory is when the title is held by the borrower with a lien to the property granted to the lender

    D. In title theory the borrower never holds the title

94. This type of loan is banned in 25 states and increases the principal balance of a loan because of a failure to make payments to the loan that covers the interest due?

    A. Conventional loan
    B. Negative amortization
    C. Unsecured loan
    D. Open-ended loan

95. Which of the following will terminate an agency in a broker-seller relationship?

    A. The owner declares bankruptcy
    B. The broker gets assistance from another broker to help sell the property
    C. The owner moves out of the property
    D. All of the above

96. Which type of community groups housing, recreation and commercial units into one self-contained development?

    A. Timeshare
    B. Mixed-use development
    C. Cooperative
    D. Planned unit development

97. A(an)_____ allows crops produced annually to be harvested from the owner or tenant who planted the crops even if the property was sold or the lease expired.

  A. Lis pendens
  B. Suit to partition
  C. Emblement
  D. Index lease

98. Which law requires lenders to disclose all loan costs to the borrower?

  A. Borrower Transparency Act
  B. Regulation Z
  C. Fair Housing Act
  D. Federal Trade Commission

99. This is the largest real estate organization in the United States.

  A. National Association of Realtors
  B. The Realtors Association
  C. United States Realtors Association
  D. None of the above

100. Which of the following factors affects real estate supply?

  A. Labor force
  B. Government controls
  C. Construction costs
  D. All of the above

101. _____ provides a history of ownership of land.

    A.   Abstract of title
    B.   Title ownership
    C.   Collusion
    D.   Property history

102. A property owner defaults on his mortgage payment, because of this the lender states that all principal installments are due immediately. What is the lender doing?

    A.   Using their power of eminent domain
    B.   Activating the acceleration clause
    C.   Dissolving the contract
    D.   The lender is not permitted to do this

103. The method of which a property owner is entitled to all that is added to the land, intentionally or by mistake, or all that the soil produces is called _____.

    A.   Blockbusting
    B.   Accession
    C.   Riparian rights
    D.   Arbitration

104. In the state of California, a _____ is a statement by an officer, i.e. notary, that states that the signatory to the instrument is acting upon their own free will.

    A.   Accretion
    B.   Acknowledgement
    C.   Accumulation
    D.   Collusion

105. What is an action to quiet title?

    A.   A lawsuit filed to remove or clear claims of another against property

    B.   A lawsuit filed by a third party to collect claims against a property

    C.   A lawsuit that has been settled outside of court

    D.   A lawsuit between a property owner and a tenant

106. When a person has direct knowledge of a real estate transaction it is called _____.

    A.   Constructive notice
    B.   Actual notice
    C.   Acknowledgement
    D.   Redlining

107. How many years of possession is required in the state of California for a person to claim adverse possession?

    A.   2 years
    B.   7 years
    C.   10 years
    D.   5 years

108. Equalizing the monthly mortgage payment over the life of the loan through the adjustment of the proportion of interest and principal is called _____.

    A.   Agency
    B.   Allodial
    C.   Amortization
    D.   Accrued interest

109. Which of the following is not required to get an appraisal license in California?

    A. 21 years of age
    B. 150 hours of education
    C. 2,000 hours of initial experience
    D. All of the above is required

110. Which organization ensure real estate appraiser as sufficiently trained and tested?

    A. National Real Estate Association
    B. National Appraisal Association
    C. Appraisal Subcommittee
    D. Housing and Urban Development

111. Who appoints the real estate commissioner in California?

    A. State governor
    B. Voted on every two years
    C. State senator
    D. Attorney general

112. What is the purpose of the California homestead laws?

    A. To provide incentive for people to buy homes
    B. To protect homeowners and property owners from losing their homes due to hardships
    C. Provide homeowners with lower interest rates if they meet the requirements
    D. None of the above

113. A property owner needs to declare _____ or more of property during a bankruptcy for the Homestead law.

A. $80,000
B. $25,000
C. $100,000
D. $75,000

114. Which type of estate can be held for an indefinite period of time?

A. Freehold estate
B. Less than freehold estate
C. Estate at sufferance
D. Estate at will

115. Which type of real estate deal occurs when there is a willing buyer and a willing seller who are knowledgeable about the market?

A. Sale by owner
B. Short sale
C. Arms-length transaction
D. Familial transaction

116. How often are the California building codes updated?

A. Every year
B. 5 years
C. 3 years
D. As needed

117. These are ordinances that are passed by the local governments that list minimum standards of the construction of buildings.

   A. New construction codes
   B. Building codes
   C. Real estate guidelines
   D. New building guidelines

118. in the state of California, who is exempt from getting a real estate license but can still sell property for a third party?

   A. The previous owner of the property
   B. A lawyer
   C. A person appointed by the court
   D. There is no exemption

119. Who administers the Cal-Vet program?

   A. State Department of Veterans
   B. Real Estate Commissioners
   C. Attorney General
   D. Department of Real Estate

120. What is the purpose of the Cal-Vet program?

   A. Provide services to military personnel currently deployed
   B. Advocate and provide services for veterans in California
   C. Buy homes for struggling veterans
   D. None of the above

121. Which California law discloses to the public the environmental effects of a discretionary project?

   A. California Environmental Quality Act
   B. National Environmental Policy Act
   C. California Environmental Policy Act
   D. Environmental Protections Act

122. What does the term "Caveat emptor" mean?

   A. Do your due diligence before selling a home
   B. For sale as is
   C. Buy at your own risk
   D. Let the buyer beware

123. Who issues a certificate of reasonable value?

   A. Department of Real Estate
   B. Real Estate Commissioner
   C. Veterans Administration
   D. Attorney General's office

124. The _____ was created to encourage research in real estate development and land use in the state of California.

   A. Real Estate Education and Research Fund
   B. Department of Real Estate
   C. Real Estate Research Committee
   D. Real Estate Research Committee

125. How can a prospective client verify a broker's license?

    A.   Through the DRE website
    B.   Through the Attorney General
    C.   Ask the broker
    D.   A client cannot verify a broker's license

126. Which type of mortgage uses personal property to secure a note?

    A.   Conventional mortgage
    B.   Chattel mortgage
    C.   Lease to own
    D.   No mortgage uses personal property

127. A _____ is needed for a developer to sell or lease any lots or parcel in a residential subdivision in California.

    A.   Subdivision public report
    B.   New residential housing report
    C.   Residential subdivision report
    D.   License to sell new property

128. Which California law acts as a consumer protection statute for potential buyers interested in buying a timeshare?

    A.   Timeshare Act of 1990
    B.   Vacation Ownership and Timeshare Act
    C.   Timeshare and Vacation Law
    D.   The Real Estate Law

129. Which documents are used to guide the development of a specific geographic area within a county or city?

A. Zoning plans
B. Parcels
C. Specific plans
D. Plottage

130. Which web-based mapping tool assists the people of Los Angeles with providing zoning information for properties within LA?

A. Zoning system
B. Zone Information and Map Access System
C. Los Angeles Zoning Access tool
D. LA zoning information tool

131. _____ are expenses accrued above the purchase prices of property and are between 2% and 5%.

A. Broker fees
B. Buyer's fees
C. Homeowners cost
D. Closing costs

132. Which of the following is not a qualification of the Cal-Vet loan?

A. Served on active duty for 90 days
B. Be honorably discharged
C. Be a resident of California
D. All of the above are qualifications

Practice Test 3

133. The _____ shows evidence of a veteran's qualification for a VA mortgage loan.

- A. Certificate of eligibility
- B. VA loan certification
- C. Cal-Vet eligibility form
- D. California loan eligibility documents

134. What is an example of commingling property in the state of California?

- A. When a married couple pool their money to buy a home without a loan
- B. When a spouse owned a home prior to the marriage and sold it to accrue a down payment on another home after marriage
- C. When one spouse pays for the mortgage on a home
- D. All of the above are examples of commingling property

135. Many California real estate projects involve _____, which is when there are common areas used by all owners, in addition to their individual living units.

- A. Subdivisions
- B. Common interest developments
- C. Condominiums
- D. Common property homes

136. Which of the following is an example of a common interest subdivision?

- A. Stock cooperatives
- B. Townhomes
- C. Vacation properties
- D. All of the above are examples

137. How does a Cal-Vet loan work?

    A. California is the lender of the loan

    B. Cal-Vet negotiates loan terms on behalf of the borrower

    C. Cal-Vet purchases the property and sells it back to the veteran

    D. Both A&C

138. Which of the following is required to get a broker license in the state of California?

    A. Be 18 years of age

    B. 2 years as a salesperson in the past 5 years

    C. Honesty

    D. All of the above

139. Which of the following is true about the license and examination fees in the state of California?

    A. The fees are not refundable

    B. Only the examination fees are refundable

    C. The examination fee is only refundable prior to taking the exam

    D. All fees are refundable

140. A realtor is advertising his home on the internet, which of the following does the realtor have to do?

    A. Indicate the sale price

    B. Indicate their license status

    C. State their real estate history

    D. All of the above

141. Which of the following does the Unruh Act discriminate from?

   A. Socio-economic status
   B. Genetic information
   C. Home size
   D. All of the above

142. In California, mortgage foreclosure consultants are required to get a certificate of registration. Which of the following is a step to get this certification?

   A. Pay a filing fee
   B. Submit an application
   C. Submit a contract that will be used with clients
   D. All of the above

143. Which statement is true regarding adverse possession in the state of California?

   A. Adverse possession does not apply if it is done in secret
   B. A family member cannot claim adverse possession
   C. The person claiming adverse possession must have paid the bulk of the mortgage
   D. All of the above are true

144. This type of license can be held by a salesperson, but the salesperson cannot perform any duties that require a license.

   A. Inactive license
   B. Dormant license
   C. Nonworking license
   D. Broker license

145. The _____ was created for consumers who have obtained a civil judgement or criminal restitution against a licensee.

    A.   California Real Estate Recovery Fund

    B.   Real Estate Research and Education Fund

    C.   Consumer Protection Fund

    D.   Consumer Recovery Fund

146. An expired license because the licensee has voluntarily canceled it or because there was a change in the corporation's status is called a(n) _____.

    A.   Expired license

    B.   Inactive license

    C.   Canceled officer

    D.   License NBA

147. How long is the Prepaid Rental Listing Service license valid for?

    A.   2 years

    B.   4 years

    C.   1 year

    D.   There is no expiration

148. Which statement is true about the PRLS license in the state of California?

    A.   The license is issued by the DRE

    B.   Anyone can get a PRLS license

    C.   Companies who are operating under a PRLS license need to maintain a $10,000 bond or cash deposit

    D.   Both A&C

149. What does the California exempt seller disclosure state?

    A.   States that some seller are exempt from special disclosures

    B.   Specific sellers are exempt from the Transfer Disclosure Statement

    C.   States that there is no exemption to the Transfer Disclosure Statement

    D.   All of the above

150. _____ is a California questionnaire that the seller is required to fill out to make the buyer aware of any material or potential issues with the property they are buying.

    A.   Seller property questionnaire

    B.   Seller notice of property to buyer form

    C.   Transfer of property questionnaire

    D.   None of the above

Answer Key

1.	A	31.	B	61.	A	91.	B	121.	A
2.	A	32.	D	62.	B	92.	A	122.	D
3.	D	33.	B	63.	A	93.	C	123.	C
4.	D	34.	A	64.	D	94.	B	124.	A
5.	D	35.	C	65.	B	95.	A	125.	A
6.	A	36.	B	66.	A	96.	D	126.	B
7.	B	37.	A	67.	C	97.	C	127.	A
8.	C	38.	D	68.	C	98.	B	128.	B
9.	C	39.	B	69.	D	99.	A	129.	A
10.	B	40.	A	70.	A	100.	D	130.	B
11.	A	41.	A	71.	A	101.	A	131.	D
12.	D	42.	C	72.	D	102.	B	132.	C
13.	D	43.	B	73.	D	103.	B	133.	A
14.	C	44.	D	74.	B	104.	B	134.	B
15.	D	45.	B	75.	D	105.	A	135.	B
16.	B	46.	C	76.	C	106.	B	136.	B
17.	C	47.	B	77.	D	107.	D	137.	D
18.	B	48.	D	78.	A	108.	C	138.	D
19.	D	49.	A	79.	D	109.	A	139.	A
20.	A	50.	A	80.	B	110.	C	140.	B
21.	C	51.	C	81.	D	111.	A	141.	B
22.	A	52.	A	82.	A	112.	B	142.	D
23.	C	53.	A	83.	C	113.	D	143.	A
24.	A	54.	D	84.	B	114.	A	144.	C
25.	B	55.	A	85.	B	115.	C	145.	A
26.	A	56.	A	86.	A	116.	D	146.	C
27.	B	57.	B	87.	D	117.	B	147.	A
28.	C	58.	A	88.	B	118.	C	148.	D
29.	C	59.	D	89.	A	119.	B	149.	B
30.	A	60.	A	90.	D	120.	B	150.	A

1. **A) Pre-approval**

Prior to purchasing a property, the borrower can visit a lender and obtain a pre-approval letter stating the amount of credit the lender is willing to accord the buyer which will help determine what the buyer can afford.

2. **A) Usable Square Footage**

Usable square footage is the amount of space you actually occupy in a leased space.

3.   **D) Principal**

The principal is the amount of money that a lender gives a borrower to facilitate property purchase. Payment of principal results in increase in borrower's equity.

4.   **D) VA mortgage**

This is a mortgage plan that is tailored to assist service members and their surviving spouses to become homeowners. There are usually a lot of qualifying standards put in place to be eligible for this type of mortgage and it is usually offered by banks and other credit facilities. The Veteran administration usually acts as a guarantor for the loan. Qualified Veterans are usually eligible for 100% financing.

5.   **D) Remaining term**

It is usually used to complete the period of time left on a loan and the amount of principal payment to be covered within that period.

6.   **A) Leaseback**

This is an arrangement that allows a seller to lease a property from the purchaser on transfer of ownership. The details surrounding the lease arrangement are usually discussed immediately after the sale.

7.   **B) Easement in gross**

Easement in gross is the agreement that attaches rights to the tenant over the property. Transfer of the land results in an immediate termination of the agreement. The agreement can be renegotiated with the new tenant over time.

8.   **C) Prepayment penalty**

This is the penalty placed on the significant payment of a mortgage within the first five years of the loan. This penalty exists to protect lenders from loss of interest income.

9.   **C) Private mortgage insurance**

These insurance payments are usually discontinued once a buyer builds up to 20% equity on the home.

10.   **B) Third party originator**

This is any third party used to originate a loan. Lenders often employ the services of third-party moderators to underwrite and originate loans. They offer no ongoing and lasting responsibility for the mortgage.

11. **A) Capital Improvement**

This is the addition of a permanent change in a structure or restoration of damaged property. It is done to increase the longevity and market value of the property. For an item to be considered a capital investment, it has to be a permanent addition and capable of improving the value of the property.

12. **D) Transfer tax**

This is any tax that is levied on transfer of ownership or title of property from one individual to another. It is usually non-deductible. It is usually levied at the local or federal level depending on the type of property changing ownership.

13. **D) All of the above**

Sales Comparison Approach, Cost Approach, and Income Approach are all appraisal methods.

14. **C) One year**

An asset must be held for at least one year before selling in order for profits to be categorized as long-term capital gains.

15. **D) All of the above**

Operating expenses include any costs associated with the operation and maintenance of an income-producing property.

16. **B) Refusing to leave a property despite expiration or termination of lease**

Commonly compared to an eviction, which is the legal removal of an individual from a lease due to violation of the terms of the agreement.

17. **C) Rate lock**

This occurs when lenders lock in a rate because it is the lowest rate being offered at the time. It is not a legally binding agreement and borrowers are allowed to abandon the rates based on the rising and falling.

18. **B) Lease option**

A lease option is a lease agreement that gives the tenant a choice to purchase the property within or at the end of the lease. It gives the buyer flexibility to make a purchase on the property. Usually involves an upfront agreement between the tenant and the landlord.

19. **D) The cooling capacity of an air conditioner and is measured in tons**

It is determined by measuring the size of the space being serviced by the air conditioner. The size area of the room is measured and multiplied by 25 BTU to determine the cooling capacity required in an air conditioner.

20. **A) Mortgage broker**

This is an individual that serves as an intermediate between lenders and brokers. A mortgage broker facilitates negotiations of interest rates and takes circulation of paperwork between the lender and the borrowers.

21. **C) $350,000**

$105,000 / 0.3 = $350,000

22. **A) Notice to cure**

This is a notice given to a leaseholder by the landlord regarding participation in activities that are not allowed in the building. The tenant is given 10 days to correct the mistake. Refusal to make adjustment results in the tenant being served a notice of termination.

23. **C) Pitch**

Defines the steepness of a roof. It is used to determine the material used for roofing and the space in the attic. It is also used to determine stability so that corrective measures can be undertaken early.

24. **A) The client**

A broker is required to work in the best interests of the client to ensure the best possible deal for the client.

25. **B) Easement**

This is the right to use another person's land temporarily without actually possessing it.

26. **A) Disabled**

Disabled, veterans, elderly, farmers, Gold Star Parents, and Star Program Homeowners. The above classes of people can get partial tax exemption by having the values of their homes reduced translating in reduced property taxes.

27. **B) 18 years**

This is the minimum required age for a real estate agent that has taken the education course and passed the qualifying exam.

28. **C) Fuse**

A fuse is a small conductor that is designed to melt under high current to break the circuit. A fuse should always maintain a series connection to the component of the circuit.

29. **C) A contract that involves both a promisor and promisee**

This contract occurs when both parties exchange a promise for a promise. Both parties enter into an agreement to fulfill their side of the bargain. Each party is also an obligor and obligee in this type of contract.

30. **A) Assessed value**

Assessed value is the monetary value assigned to a property and is usually used to determine the value of a property for the purpose of taxation.

31. **B) Environmental Protection Agency**

The Environmental Protection Agency is tasked with protecting both human and environmental health. The agency creates standards and laws promoting health of individuals and the environment and participates in upholding them by administering correcting efforts like CERCLA.

32. **D) Pro Forma Statement**

This is an estimate summary of income production if the current trends are maintained. This is usually in multifamily properties in order to help the investor understand general financial operations of the property.

33. **B) Create record of refusal in writing**

In the case where a client refuses to sign a disclosure, the agent is required to clearly state the names of the client and the facts surrounding the refusal to sign the disclosure. An agent is also required to sign a declaration in the presence of a notary public and have it notarized.

34. **A) Mortgage**

A voluntary lien is a claim a debtor has over the property of another and is initiated by the debtor as in the case of a mortgage. The debtor cannot legally sell the property as it is considered collateral.

35.   **C) Broker**

An agent resorts to a broker for commission as the law does not allow salespersons to work independently and therefore cannot be paid directly. A broker on receiving commission from the sale of the property is required to split the commission amongst the agents that were involved in the transaction.

36.   **B) Ownership in severalty**

This is a situation where real estate is owned by a single person or entity providing the owner with the most control of the land. A sole owner is at will to take any action on the land such as selling or leasing.

37.   **A) People who pose as real estate clients to check if fair housing is being practiced**

Testing was initiated under the Fair Housing Act to ensure that housing providers act in accordance with the fair housing laws that protect against discrimination based on race, origin and gender.

38.   **D) Accretion**

This is the natural growth of a parcel of land due to mother nature. It occurs due to accumulation of soil on the shoreline of a water body. A decrease due to erosion is also possible.

39.   **B) 27.5 years**

Depreciation is the loss of value of a property due to age, wear and tear. A residential property can only declare depreciation after 27.5 years in order to reduce the value of the property and property tax on the property.

40.   **A) Chattel**

A chattel is a tangible property which is either mobile or immobile. However, this term cannot be used to describe real estate holdings.

41.   **A) RESPA**

The Real Estate Settling Procedures Act was developed in order to protect the parties involved in a real estate transaction from abuse during the settlement process. The act mandates lenders and brokers to disclose all matters crucial to the transaction service, settlement service and consumer protection laws

42. **C) Percolation**

This is the process in which water reaches the subsoil and roots. The pore space present in soil acts as a medium for the water to percolate. The ability of water to move through soil is dependent on the soil texture and structure. Some soils allow water to move very deep into the ground which may result in mixing with underground water reservoirs.

43. **B) Passive income**

This is income that is generated with minimal activity. It requires little to no effort to earn on a daily basis.

44. **D) Straight term mortgage**

A straight term mortgage is a mortgage that allows the mortgagor to make monthly payments on the interest accrued throughout the mortgage's lifespan. The principal remains unpaid until a set date where it becomes due for payment in full.

45. **B) Dual agent**

Mary's agent was able to perform the above transactions for her because he was working for both the Mary and the seller of the property.

46. **C) Metes and bounds**

This is a legal principle of land description and uses natural and artificial landmarks as boundaries. It is often used to describe irregular tracts of land. Metes defines straight line distances while bounds defines a less regular but identifiable lines. Measurements from an original point that is a monument and metes and bounds are described taking into account the boundaries. The process is repeated until the surveyor returns to the original point.

47. **B) Wraparound mortgage**

Wraparound mortgages are used to refinance property. They are mini loans that include the balance of the preexisting mortgage and an additional loan to cover the new property. The seller is granted a promissory note highlighting the amount due.

48. **D) Real estate agents and brokers**

They need to be licensed as they legally represent clients, buyers and sellers, in transferring ownership of property.

49. **A) Commingling**

This is a breach of trust that occurs when a representative of a client mixes individual funds with that of the client making it impossible to determine the amounts that belong to each individual.

50.   **A) They decrease**

Money supply is influenced by supply and demand. An increase in the money supply will result in a decreased interest rate making it easier to borrow and vice versa. Therefore, money and interest rates have an inversely proportional relationship.

51.   **C) HO3**

A home owner's policy is a property insurance that covers losses and damages done to the insured's house and assets within the home. It also provides liability coverage against accidents within the home.

52.   **A) Ad valorem tax**

This is the tax levied by a municipality or local government entity based on assessed value. A public assessor is engaged to value the property in order to calculate the tax owed.

53.   **A) Gross lease**

This is a flat rent fee that included all expenses associated with ownership. It is inclusive of incidental charges such as taxes, insurance and utilities. It is an uncommon lease as landlords are unaware of the utility charges that may be incurred by a tenant.

54.   **D) None of the above**

$442,000 / (1 - 0.05) = $465,263

55.   **A) Bridge Loan**

This is a short-term loan of up to one year that provides cash flow enabling an individual to meet current obligations while awaiting permanent financing. It is often used in real estate to purchase a new home while awaiting the sale of the old property.

56.   **A) House rules**

These are set rules that have been put in place to ensure the comfort of the tenants living within the building. Violation of the house rules clause may result in eviction.

57.   **B) Lessee**

The original tenant for rent as he/she is liable to the owner. In case of overdue rent by the new tenant, the original tenant is held accountable.

58.   **A) Active income**

This is an income earned from performing services. Active participation is required to yield payment.

59. **D) Leasehold estate**

This is a lease that allows the tenant to have real property for an extended period of time. A time frame is agreed upon in the lease and the tenant is allowed to erect structures and profit from the business that has been established at the site.

60. **A) Certificate of occupancy**

This is a legal statement issued by the building department clearing a building for occupancy on meeting the building codes and other laws that surround the construction of a residential or commercial building. It can be obtained when a new building is constructed or an old building is repurposed.

61. **A) Amortized loan**

An amortized loan is a loan with a scheduled payment over a period of time that pays off the interest and principal. An amortized loan payment schedule focuses on paying off the interest and progresses into the principal.

62. **B) Net operating income**

This is a method used to value the income generating properties. To obtain the value, all expenses incurred during operations is subtracted to the total income produced by the property. To get the true value produced by the property, revenues earned must be included.

63. **A) Graduated lease**

A graduated lease is an agreement between the landlord and tenant that allows for periodic adjustment of monthly payments based on the market value of the property. It stands to benefit the landlord over a long period of time.

64. **D) $500,000**

In accordance with the Taxpayers Relief Act, a married couple is eligible for exclusion from capital gain tax for profits of up to $500,000. This is provided the property sold is a primary residence, they have been living in it for at least 2 years.

65. **B) Carry a physical copy or have a digital image on a device**

A pocket card is a pocket-sized license identifying the holder as a licensed agent. It contains a photo, name and business address of the holder.

66. **A) Attorney**

This is licensed broker that engages the services of other agents with intentions of splitting commission paid on the sale of a property.

67. **C) $250,000**

According to the Taxpayers relief act, a single person is eligible for a capital gains tax exemption for profits of up to $250,000 on the sale of a primary home.

68. **C) Encroachment**

Encroachment is a violation of property rights that occurs when an individual chooses to ignore set boundaries. This can be by extending structure into the neighbor's land or illegally entering the neighbor's property.

69. **D) HO4**

This insurance is designed to protect the insured and belongings from the covered losses. It covers liability, personal property, additional living expenses and medical payments to others. The insurance covers against risks specified in the policy.

70. **A) Tenancy in common**

A tenancy in common is a legal agreement where two or more people with undivided rights own a property. Members of a tenancy in common are not mandated to have equal rights and can enter the agreement at any time. Members of a tenancy in common are free to leave their shares to a beneficiary.

71. **A) Deed**

This is a signed legal document that conveys interest of a property and is used in cases of transfer of property provided a set of conditions are met. For a deed to hold legal merit, it must be filed in a public record.

72. **D) Chain of title**

This is an official ownership record of a property. It is usually maintained from a centralized registry. It is used widely to protect lenders and buyers from losses occurring due to errors in the title report.

73. **D) 24%**

($4,000 * 12) / $200,000 = 0.24

74. **B) Certificate that is presented by veterans to show proof that they have met the minimum service requirements to be eligible for a VA loan**

The Certificate of Eligibility serves as proof of a veteran's military service and must be provided to lenders during the VA loan process

75. **D) Title insurance**

A title insurance is based on the indemnity clause. It is taken by a buyer to protect the lender from loss caused by unidentified defects in the title. It acts against traditional insurance by protecting clients against claims on a past occurrence

76. **C) Time-share**

Also called vacation ownership, a time-share is shared ownership of a property. This type of property is typically a vacation property i.e. a condominium in a resort area. The buyer typically purchases a certain period of time for the unit, typically one- to two-week periods.

77. **D) Real estate that is purchased by a group which includes at least one sponsor and several investors**

Syndication is a method investors can use to invest in properties. Investors pool their financial and intellectual resources together to invest in properties that they would not be able to invest in individually.

78. **A) Notarized signature**

A notarized signature is not necessary in a contract. A legal purpose, competent parties, offer and acceptance, consideration and consent are the essential elements of a contract.

79. **D) Both A and C**

Exclusive agency listing is an agreement between a real estate firm and seller which grants the firm the exclusive rights to sell the property but also allows the seller to sell the home without paying a commission to the listing agent. An open listing is a property listing using multiple real estate agents. This type of listing also allows an owner to list and sell the property without paying a commission to an agent.

80. **B) Exclusive-right-to-sell listing**

A legal agreement under which the seller agrees to pay a commission to the listing broker. The listing broker acts as the agent and is provided commission whether the property is sold through the listing broker, seller or anyone else. An exception occurs when the seller names one or more individuals/entities as exemptions in the listing agreement.

81. **D) All of the above**

Functional obsolescence occurs when an objects usefulness or desirability has been reduced because of an outdated design feature. They are features that cannot be easily fixed.

82. **A) Interstate Land Sales Full Disclosure Act**

Passed in 1968, this act protects against land scams by facilitating the regulation of interstate land sales. Developers need to register subdivisions that contain more than 100 or more nonexempt lots. They may also provide purchasers with a disclosure statement (property report) prior to a sale.

83. **C) Re-zoning of a property**

A seller is required to disclose all known material facts regarding the property to a buyer. Personal information about the family is not required but a re-zoning of the property must be disclosed.

84. **B) Special assessment tax**

Property owners are sometimes taxed for improvements that effect some of the property owners within a taxing district. Only the property owners who have been affected will be taxed. These taxes pay for local infrastructure projects such as sewer lines, or construction and maintenance of roads.

85. **B) Price-fixing**

Price-fixing, boycotting and allocation of customer or markets are the most common anti-trust violations in real estate.

86. **A) Involuntary alienation**

This type of alienation results from a levy and sale for taxes that are due from the owner. It can also result from bankruptcy or an insolvency.

87. **D) All of the above**

A fiduciary duty is an obligation to act in the best interest of the principal. There are 6 common law duties care, obedience, loyalty, disclosure, accounting and confidentiality.

88. **B) Graduated lease**

This type of lease allows the landlord to a periodic adjustment of monthly payments. An increase in monthly payments could be due to market conditions or because of increase in the value of leased property.

89. **A) Variance**

A variance is a request to deviate from current zoning requirements. It allows the owner to use a piece of land in a way that it is not usually permitted by the zoning ordinance. It is a waiver and does not change the zoning law.

90.   **D) Latent defect**

A latent defect is a fault in a property that cannot be found through a reasonable inspection prior to a sale. These hazards may jeopardize the structural integrity or the occupant's safety.

91.   **B) The buyer is required to buy the property once the option agreement has been completed**

In an option to buy agreement the buyer needs to purchase the property if the optionee agrees to the contract. The optionee is not required accept the buyers offer.

92.   **A) Federal Housing Administration loan**

The FHA loan is designed for low to moderate borrowers and require a lower minimum down payments and credit score than other conventional loans. This type of loan is issued by an approved lender and insured by the FHA.

93.   **C) Lien theory is when the title is held by the borrower with a lien to the property granted to the lender**

The difference between lien theory and title theory is that in lien theory the buyer holds the deed while in title theory the lender holds the title until the final payment is made.

94.   **B) Negative amortization**

Negative amortization is banned in 25 states and is considered predatory by the federal government. It refers to increasing the principal balance of a loan due to the failure to cover the interest that is due on that loan.

95.   **A) The owner declares bankruptcy**

When a property owner declares bankruptcy the agency agreement is terminated. If the principal passes, then the agreement is also terminated. Getting help from other brokers and moving out of the property are not means for termination.

96.   **D) Planned unit development**

The planned unit development is a type of development that has varied, and compatible land uses i.e. housing, recreations and commercial centers.

97.   **C) Emblements**

Emblements are considered personal property. It allows whoever planted the crops the ability to harvest them no matter who owns the property.

98.   **B) Regulation Z**

This law gives the borrowers the right to cancel certain credit transactions. This law is also called the Truth-in-Lending Laws.

99.   **A) National Association of Realtors**

The NAR is an organization of real estate brokers that was created to promote the profession and foster professional behavior to its members. It has its own code of ethics that all members are required to adhere to.

100.   **D) All of the above**

All of the above factors affect the supply of real estate. The government financial policies will also affect the supply of real estate.

101.   **A) Abstract of title**

An abstract of title is a list of transfers of titles, rights and liabilities on a specific parcel of land. It consists of a summary of the original grant and the subsequent conveyances and encumbrances that affect the property. It also provides a certification by an abstractor which states the history is complete and accurate.

102.   **B) Activating the acceleration clause**

The acceleration clause is a provision in a contract that states that if the borrower does not meet specified requirements, then the borrower needs to repay all of an outstanding loan.

103.   **B) Accession**

Accession is property law that states a method of acquiring property is by adding value to other property through labor or raw materials. Ownership of property is naturally carried with its right to possess all things that have been added or produced by the property.

104.   **B) Acknowledgement**

This is a formal declaration that has been made in front of a witness, i.e. notary, stating that the execution of an instrument was their own free-will.

105.   **A) A lawsuit filed to remove or clear claims of another against property**

A quiet title action is a lawsuit to establish their title against an adverse claim. The interest in the land can be the title to the property, an easement, a license, a lease, or title by adverse possession.

106. **B) Actual notice**

Actual notice is when a person has been given direct notice of an existing case that might affect their interests. There are two types of actual notice express actual notice and implied actual notice.

107. **D) 5 years**

5 years of possession and payment of taxes throughout the 5-year period is required for eligibility for a legal title in the state of California.

108. **C) Amortization**

Amortization is a method of equalizing monthly mortgage payments, where at first the interest payment is high, and the principal payment is low.

109. **A) 21 years of age**

A person needs to be at least 18 years of age to become a residential real estate appraiser. They must also pass and exam and pay a fee.

110. **C) Appraisal Subcommittee**

This is a national organization that ensures competency and independent judgement of appraisers are meeting the standards listed. They monitor the states on licensing and certifications of real property appraisers.

111. **A) State governor**

The commissioner is appointed by the state governor and is responsible for overseeing the licensing and behavior of California licenses and over 300 staff.

112. **B) To protect homeowners and property owners from losing their homes due to hardships**

The homestead act is a protection for homeowners and small property owners who are going through a hardship. There are a specified set of requirements they must meet in order to qualify.

113. **D) $75,000**

The property owner must declare $75,000+ worth of their property as a protected homestead during a bankruptcy proceeding.

114. **A) Freehold estate**

This type of estate gives the owner exclusive rights to enjoy the property for an undefined length of time.

115. **C) Arms-length transaction**

In this type of transaction, the buyer and the seller act independently without another party's influence. The amount that is charged needs to be the same as it would be on an open market.

116. **D) 3 years**

The building codes are updated and shared with the public every three years and it includes supplemental information. The most recent version was published in 2020.

117. **B) Building codes**

These regulations govern the design, construction, maintenance and alteration of structures. There are minimum requirements put in place to ensure the health, safety and welfare of the occupants.

118. **C) A person appointed by the court**

Anyone who is appointed by the court of law is exempt from licensure. An owner has the right to sell their own property, but no other exemptions exist.

119. **B) State Department of Veterans**

The State Department of Veterans is responsible for administering the Cal-Vet program. The program assists in the direct financing of farm and home purchases.

120. **B) Advocate and provide services for veterans in California**

This program offers services to honorably discharged veterans and helps veterans connect with the right benefits.

121. **A) California Environmental Quality Act**

This law provides procedures and information that ensures governmental agencies consider and respond to environmental effects of their decisions.

122. **D) Let the buyer beware**

The buyer needs to do their due diligence before they decide to make a purchase. This term is typically used in real property transactions

123. **C) Veterans Administration**

The certification is used by the Veterans Administration to certify that the value of the property has been secured by a VA mortgage appraisal.

124. **A) Real Estate Education and Research Fund**

This fund was created to promote real estate and land research. 8% of real estate license fees is used to finance the fund.

125. **A) Through the DRE website**

A client can verify a license in California by searching the company name, licensee or license ID through the DRE website.

126. **B) Chattel mortgage**

The chattel mortgage is an arrangement in which personal property acts as security of a loan. This guarantees a loan and the lender holds an interest in the property.

127. **A) Subdivision public report**

The Business and Professions Code 11018.2 states that no one can sell or lease lots or parcels in a residential subdivision without this report in the state of California.

128. **B) Vacation Ownership and Timeshare Act**

This California law is a consumer protection statute that provides regulations against the salesman and the content found in an offering brochure.

129. **A) Zoning plans**

These are planning documents that help to guide development in certain areas such as counties and cities. New development or subdivisions need to be consistent with the specific plan.

130. **B) Zone Information and Map Access System**

ZIMAS is a tool that assists people in finding zoning information for Los Angeles. LA city planning developed this tool to help businesses and residents make informed decisions about land use.

131. **D) Closing costs**

These are the expenses accrued above the purchase price of a property. These costs can include attorney fees, title searches, taxes, lender costs and more.

132. **C) Be a resident of California**

There are no rules regarding residency for the Cal-Vet loan, those who were on active duty for training purposes, during wartime or peacetime are all eligible.

133. **A) Certificate of eligibility**

This document is the beginning of the VA loan process and shows that the lender meets the service requirement to obtain the loan.

134. **B) When a spouse owned a home prior to the marriage and sold it to accrue a down payment on another home after marriage.**

In this case the down payment on the home is considered separate property because it came from a home owned by one spouse prior to marriage. When a couple divorces this will be accounted for when the value of the property is split.

135. **B) Common interest developments**

This type of property is one in which the property owners have rights to various common areas as well as the premises they own. The HOA has power to regulate the property and collect fees from the members.

136. **B) Stock cooperatives**

Common interest subdivisions are land that includes a common interest in property with others and a separate interest in property. This can be through an association. Another example is a condominium.

137. **D) Both A&C**

California is the lender in this type of loan. Cal-Vet buys the property and then sells it back to the veteran through a land contract or a contract of sale.

138. **D) All of the above**

All of the above is required to become a broker in the state of California. Non-residents must fill out a separate form to apply for a broker license.

139. **A) The fees are not refundable**

The examination and licensing fees are not refundable in the state of California.

140. **B) Indicate their license status**

The licensee must state their license status if they would like to advertise on the internet, according to B&P sections 10235.5 and 10140.6

141. **B) Genetic information**

The Unruh Act outlaws discrimination against sex, race, color, religion, ancestry, national origin, age, disability, medical condition, genetic information, marital status, and sexual orientation.

142. **D) All of the above**

All of the above is required and needs to be submitted to the California Attorney General's office to receive a certificate of registrations.

143. **A) Adverse possession does not apply if it is done in secret**

California requires that possession of property must occur openly in order to qualify for adverse possession.

144. **C) Nonworking license**

A person who carries this type of license cannot work as a salesperson in the state of California until their license is reactivated.

145. **A) California Real Estate Recovery Fund**

This fund was created in 1964 and is funded by the license and fees collected by real estate agents. It is used to pay for restitution against a licensee because of fraud or other grounds.

146. **C) Canceled officer**

This type of real estate license is expired because the licensee has voluntarily canceled it or due to a change in the corporation's status.

147. **A) 2 years**

The license lasts for 2 years and must be renewed in order for the licensee to engage in PRLS services.

148. **D) Both A&C**

Both are true regarding the PRLS license in the state of California. The license is required when supplying tenants with listings of residential real property for rent.

149. **B) Specific sellers are exempt from the Transfer Disclosure Statement**

The TDS form is needed when the Seller Property Questionnaire is required. Foreclosure sales and court order transfers are two reasons when the TDS is not needed.

150.   **A) Seller property questionnaire**

The seller property questionnaire or SPQ is a requirement by the state of California that needs to be filled out by the seller prior to a property sale.

Practice Test 4

Directions:

1. You have 3 hours to complete the exam.

2. To pass, you must answer at least 105 out of 150 questions correctly.

3. Some questions will require mathematics. You may use a calculator.

4. **Phones and pagers are not allowed. Having either will result in automatic dismissal from the exam and nullification of exam scores.**

Tips:

- Answer all questions even if you are unsure.
- Mark any questions you are stuck on and revisit them after you are done. The exam is timed so make sure you finish as many questions as you can.
- After reading the question, try answering it in your head first to avoid getting confused by the choices.
- Read the entire question before looking at the answers.
- Use the process of elimination to filter out choices that don't seem correct to increase your chances of selecting the correct answer.
- Be aware of important keywords like **not, sometimes, always,** and **never**. These words completely alter the ask of the question so it's important to keep track of them.

PLEASE READ THESE INSTRUCTIONS CAREFULLY.

Practice Test 4

Name: _____   Date: _____

1.	Ⓐ Ⓑ Ⓒ Ⓓ	31.	Ⓐ Ⓑ Ⓒ Ⓓ	61.	Ⓐ Ⓑ Ⓒ Ⓓ
2.	Ⓐ Ⓑ Ⓒ Ⓓ	32.	Ⓐ Ⓑ Ⓒ Ⓓ	62.	Ⓐ Ⓑ Ⓒ Ⓓ
3.	Ⓐ Ⓑ Ⓒ Ⓓ	33.	Ⓐ Ⓑ Ⓒ Ⓓ	63.	Ⓐ Ⓑ Ⓒ Ⓓ
4.	Ⓐ Ⓑ Ⓒ Ⓓ	34.	Ⓐ Ⓑ Ⓒ Ⓓ	64.	Ⓐ Ⓑ Ⓒ Ⓓ
5.	Ⓐ Ⓑ Ⓒ Ⓓ	35.	Ⓐ Ⓑ Ⓒ Ⓓ	65.	Ⓐ Ⓑ Ⓒ Ⓓ
6.	Ⓐ Ⓑ Ⓒ Ⓓ	36.	Ⓐ Ⓑ Ⓒ Ⓓ	66.	Ⓐ Ⓑ Ⓒ Ⓓ
7.	Ⓐ Ⓑ Ⓒ Ⓓ	37.	Ⓐ Ⓑ Ⓒ Ⓓ	67.	Ⓐ Ⓑ Ⓒ Ⓓ
8.	Ⓐ Ⓑ Ⓒ Ⓓ	38.	Ⓐ Ⓑ Ⓒ Ⓓ	68.	Ⓐ Ⓑ Ⓒ Ⓓ
9.	Ⓐ Ⓑ Ⓒ Ⓓ	39.	Ⓐ Ⓑ Ⓒ Ⓓ	69.	Ⓐ Ⓑ Ⓒ Ⓓ
10.	Ⓐ Ⓑ Ⓒ Ⓓ	40.	Ⓐ Ⓑ Ⓒ Ⓓ	70.	Ⓐ Ⓑ Ⓒ Ⓓ
11.	Ⓐ Ⓑ Ⓒ Ⓓ	41.	Ⓐ Ⓑ Ⓒ Ⓓ	71.	Ⓐ Ⓑ Ⓒ Ⓓ
12.	Ⓐ Ⓑ Ⓒ Ⓓ	42.	Ⓐ Ⓑ Ⓒ Ⓓ	72.	Ⓐ Ⓑ Ⓒ Ⓓ
13.	Ⓐ Ⓑ Ⓒ Ⓓ	43.	Ⓐ Ⓑ Ⓒ Ⓓ	73.	Ⓐ Ⓑ Ⓒ Ⓓ
14.	Ⓐ Ⓑ Ⓒ Ⓓ	44.	Ⓐ Ⓑ Ⓒ Ⓓ	74.	Ⓐ Ⓑ Ⓒ Ⓓ
15.	Ⓐ Ⓑ Ⓒ Ⓓ	45.	Ⓐ Ⓑ Ⓒ Ⓓ	75.	Ⓐ Ⓑ Ⓒ Ⓓ
16.	Ⓐ Ⓑ Ⓒ Ⓓ	46.	Ⓐ Ⓑ Ⓒ Ⓓ	76.	Ⓐ Ⓑ Ⓒ Ⓓ
17	Ⓐ Ⓑ Ⓒ Ⓓ	47.	Ⓐ Ⓑ Ⓒ Ⓓ	77.	Ⓐ Ⓑ Ⓒ Ⓓ
18.	Ⓐ Ⓑ Ⓒ Ⓓ	48.	Ⓐ Ⓑ Ⓒ Ⓓ	78.	Ⓐ Ⓑ Ⓒ Ⓓ
19.	Ⓐ Ⓑ Ⓒ Ⓓ	49.	Ⓐ Ⓑ Ⓒ Ⓓ	79.	Ⓐ Ⓑ Ⓒ Ⓓ
20.	Ⓐ Ⓑ Ⓒ Ⓓ	50.	Ⓐ Ⓑ Ⓒ Ⓓ	80.	Ⓐ Ⓑ Ⓒ Ⓓ
21.	Ⓐ Ⓑ Ⓒ Ⓓ	51.	Ⓐ Ⓑ Ⓒ Ⓓ	81.	Ⓐ Ⓑ Ⓒ Ⓓ
22.	Ⓐ Ⓑ Ⓒ Ⓓ	52.	Ⓐ Ⓑ Ⓒ Ⓓ	82.	Ⓐ Ⓑ Ⓒ Ⓓ
23.	Ⓐ Ⓑ Ⓒ Ⓓ	53.	Ⓐ Ⓑ Ⓒ Ⓓ	83.	Ⓐ Ⓑ Ⓒ Ⓓ
24.	Ⓐ Ⓑ Ⓒ Ⓓ	54.	Ⓐ Ⓑ Ⓒ Ⓓ	84.	Ⓐ Ⓑ Ⓒ Ⓓ
25.	Ⓐ Ⓑ Ⓒ Ⓓ	55.	Ⓐ Ⓑ Ⓒ Ⓓ	85.	Ⓐ Ⓑ Ⓒ Ⓓ
26.	Ⓐ Ⓑ Ⓒ Ⓓ	56.	Ⓐ Ⓑ Ⓒ Ⓓ	86.	Ⓐ Ⓑ Ⓒ Ⓓ
27.	Ⓐ Ⓑ Ⓒ Ⓓ	57.	Ⓐ Ⓑ Ⓒ Ⓓ	87.	Ⓐ Ⓑ Ⓒ Ⓓ
28.	Ⓐ Ⓑ Ⓒ Ⓓ	58.	Ⓐ Ⓑ Ⓒ Ⓓ	88.	Ⓐ Ⓑ Ⓒ Ⓓ
29.	Ⓐ Ⓑ Ⓒ Ⓓ	59.	Ⓐ Ⓑ Ⓒ Ⓓ	89.	Ⓐ Ⓑ Ⓒ Ⓓ
30.	Ⓐ Ⓑ Ⓒ Ⓓ	60.	Ⓐ Ⓑ Ⓒ Ⓓ	90.	Ⓐ Ⓑ Ⓒ Ⓓ

Name: _____   Date: _____

91.	Ⓐ Ⓑ Ⓒ Ⓓ	121.	Ⓐ Ⓑ Ⓒ Ⓓ
92.	Ⓐ Ⓑ Ⓒ Ⓓ	122.	Ⓐ Ⓑ Ⓒ Ⓓ
93.	Ⓐ Ⓑ Ⓒ Ⓓ	123.	Ⓐ Ⓑ Ⓒ Ⓓ
94.	Ⓐ Ⓑ Ⓒ Ⓓ	124.	Ⓐ Ⓑ Ⓒ Ⓓ
95.	Ⓐ Ⓑ Ⓒ Ⓓ	125.	Ⓐ Ⓑ Ⓒ Ⓓ
96.	Ⓐ Ⓑ Ⓒ Ⓓ	126.	Ⓐ Ⓑ Ⓒ Ⓓ
97.	Ⓐ Ⓑ Ⓒ Ⓓ	127.	Ⓐ Ⓑ Ⓒ Ⓓ
98.	Ⓐ Ⓑ Ⓒ Ⓓ	128.	Ⓐ Ⓑ Ⓒ Ⓓ
99.	Ⓐ Ⓑ Ⓒ Ⓓ	129.	Ⓐ Ⓑ Ⓒ Ⓓ
100.	Ⓐ Ⓑ Ⓒ Ⓓ	130.	Ⓐ Ⓑ Ⓒ Ⓓ
101.	Ⓐ Ⓑ Ⓒ Ⓓ	131.	Ⓐ Ⓑ Ⓒ Ⓓ
102.	Ⓐ Ⓑ Ⓒ Ⓓ	132.	Ⓐ Ⓑ Ⓒ Ⓓ
103.	Ⓐ Ⓑ Ⓒ Ⓓ	133.	Ⓐ Ⓑ Ⓒ Ⓓ
104.	Ⓐ Ⓑ Ⓒ Ⓓ	134.	Ⓐ Ⓑ Ⓒ Ⓓ
105.	Ⓐ Ⓑ Ⓒ Ⓓ	135.	Ⓐ Ⓑ Ⓒ Ⓓ
106.	Ⓐ Ⓑ Ⓒ Ⓓ	136.	Ⓐ Ⓑ Ⓒ Ⓓ
107	Ⓐ Ⓑ Ⓒ Ⓓ	137.	Ⓐ Ⓑ Ⓒ Ⓓ
108.	Ⓐ Ⓑ Ⓒ Ⓓ	138.	Ⓐ Ⓑ Ⓒ Ⓓ
109.	Ⓐ Ⓑ Ⓒ Ⓓ	139.	Ⓐ Ⓑ Ⓒ Ⓓ
110.	Ⓐ Ⓑ Ⓒ Ⓓ	140.	Ⓐ Ⓑ Ⓒ Ⓓ
111.	Ⓐ Ⓑ Ⓒ Ⓓ	141.	Ⓐ Ⓑ Ⓒ Ⓓ
112.	Ⓐ Ⓑ Ⓒ Ⓓ	142.	Ⓐ Ⓑ Ⓒ Ⓓ
113.	Ⓐ Ⓑ Ⓒ Ⓓ	143.	Ⓐ Ⓑ Ⓒ Ⓓ
114.	Ⓐ Ⓑ Ⓒ Ⓓ	144.	Ⓐ Ⓑ Ⓒ Ⓓ
115.	Ⓐ Ⓑ Ⓒ Ⓓ	145.	Ⓐ Ⓑ Ⓒ Ⓓ
116.	Ⓐ Ⓑ Ⓒ Ⓓ	146.	Ⓐ Ⓑ Ⓒ Ⓓ
117.	Ⓐ Ⓑ Ⓒ Ⓓ	147.	Ⓐ Ⓑ Ⓒ Ⓓ
118.	Ⓐ Ⓑ Ⓒ Ⓓ	148.	Ⓐ Ⓑ Ⓒ Ⓓ
119.	Ⓐ Ⓑ Ⓒ Ⓓ	149.	Ⓐ Ⓑ Ⓒ Ⓓ
120.	Ⓐ Ⓑ Ⓒ Ⓓ	150.	Ⓐ Ⓑ Ⓒ Ⓓ

1. Which of the following is considered commercial real estate?

   A. Office building
   B. Warehouse
   C. Multifamily house
   D. All of the above

2. Jack is trying to convince Mary to move to a particular neighborhood because the residents there are of her ethnic background and religion. What is guilty of?

   A. Blockbusting
   B. Discriminating
   C. Convincing
   D. Steering

3. What type of lease would a tenant take when using a warehouse for the purpose of manufacturing and distribution?

   A. Gross lease
   B. Net lease
   C. Percentage lease
   D. Proprietary lease

4. What is a notice given on a pending lawsuit?

   A. Lis Pendens
   B. Statute of limitations
   C. Notice of intent
   D. Notice of default

5. Who issues variances?

   A. Architectural Review Board
   B. EPA
   C. Municipal Engineers
   D. Zoning Board of Appeals

6. What is the name given to an individual who originates, sells and services mortgage loans?

   A. Mortgage Banker
   B. Mortgage Broker
   C. Lender
   D. Borrower

7. What is the exterior layer of a house?

   A. Eaves
   B. Flashing
   C. Pitch
   D. Sheathing

8. Who holds on to the security deposit?

   A. Agent
   B. Broker
   C. Buyer
   D. Landlord

Practice Test 4

9. What is the term used to define the estimated age of a property based on its utilities and physical wear and tear?

   A. Economic life
   B. Effective age
   C. Use discount
   D. Depreciation

10. How long are brokers required to hold on to property files?

   A. One year
   B. Three years
   C. Five years
   D. Never

11. What is the unit used to measure furnace or air conditioner capacity?

   A. British Thermal Unit
   B. Bytes
   C. Joules
   D. Watts

12. What describes the type of estate granted within a lease?

   A. Acceleration clause
   B. Annuity law
   C. Cancellation clause
   D. Habendum clause

13. What type of income is income generated from a rental property?

   A. Active
   B. Passive
   C. Portfolio
   D. All the above

14. What is another name used to refer to land lease?

   A. Ground lease
   B. Home lease
   C. Percentage lease
   D. Estate lease

15. Which regulations govern the construction details of buildings with the sole interest of safeguarding the occupants and general public?

   A. APR
   B. Building codes
   C. Leasing laws
   D. Zoning codes

16. If a seller nets $325,000 from the sale of her home, and the commission is 3%, how much did the home sell for?

   A. $334,750
   B. $335,051
   C. $315,250
   D. $334,027

17. Personal property that is attached to real property, such as a chandelier, is regarded as

    A.   An emblement
    B.   An appliance
    C.   A fixture
    D.   A liability

18. What are outside amenities that maximize use of property called?

    A.   Cosmetic improvements
    B.   Essential improvements
    C.   Offsite improvements
    D.   Supplemental improvements

19. Which form of ownership passes the shares of ownership upon death?

    A.   Life estate
    B.   Severalty
    C.   Tenancy in common
    D.   Joint tenancy

20. If a property manager is fixing a leaky pipe, what type of maintenance is he doing?

    A.   Aesthetic maintenance
    B.   Appreciation
    C.   Breakdown prevention
    D.   Preventive maintenance

21. Which act was enacted in order to identify hazardous sites?

    A.   Americans with disabilities Act
    B.   CERCLA
    C.   Fair Housing Act
    D.   Civil Rights Act

22. What is tenancy in common?

    A.   A shared tenancy in which each holder has a distinct, separately transferable interest
    B.   A tenancy in which each holder has equal interest, where interest is automatically passed in case of death
    C.   A tenancy in which interest is returned to the public upon death
    D.   A tenancy in which a single owner owns full ownership of a property

23. What is the money available after deducting all expenses?

    A.   Cash out returns
    B.   Cash flow
    C.   Cash on cash return
    D.   Revenue

24. What is an involuntary lien?

    A.   A lien that arises without the property owner's consent
    B.   A lien that is initiated with owner's consent
    C.   A lien that cannot be cashed on
    D.   None of the above

25. What is the name given to property that legally qualifies as owner's principal property?

    A. Commercial property
    B. Homestead property
    C. Real property
    D. Personal property

26. A person authorized to handle a principal's affairs in one specific area is referred to as?

    A. General agent
    B. Dual agent
    C. Multi agent
    D. Special agent

27. What are real property rights conferred with ownership?

    A. Bundle of rights
    B. Right of first refusal
    C. Riparian rights
    D. Doctrine of equitable conversion

28. What is the fine placed for a violation of license law?

    A. $1,000
    B. $5,000
    C. $6,000
    D. $10,000

29. What is the term for commercial property depreciation?

    A. 5 years
    B. 29 years
    C. 39 years
    D. 40 years

30. The division of expenses at the time of closing between the buyer and seller in proportion to the actual use of a property is called?

    A. Bill of sale
    B. Loan to value ratio
    C. Proration
    D. Tax abatement

31. What is the equivalent of 1 cubic foot?

    A. 5.25 gallons
    B. 7.26 gallons
    C. 7.48 gallons
    D. 10 gallons

32. What is a statement that shows total revenues generated based on rent rolls and management styles?

    A. Invoice statement
    B. Income statement
    C. Pro forma statement
    D. Operating statement

33. What type of building is divided into two condominiums where the first is the co-op residential units (80%) and the second is for professional/commercial units (20%)?

    A.   Condo
    B.   Condop
    C.   Co-op
    D.   Multi family home

34. A person authorized to handle a principal's affairs in more than one specific area is referred to as?

    A.   Special agent
    B.   General Agent
    C.   Dual agent
    D.   Broker

35. What are the laws that limit the maximum interest rate that can be charged?

    A.   APR
    B.   Annuity laws
    C.   FHA
    D.   Usury

36. What is the nature of the title in co-op ownership?

    A.   Freehold
    B.   Leasehold
    C.   Regular hold
    D.   Lease assignment

37. What is a non-possessory interest in property giving a lienholder the right to foreclose?

    A.   Mortgage
    B.   Duties
    C.   Taxes
    D.   Revenue

38. What is the agreement that allows the tenant to continue living on a property once the lease has expired?

    A.   Tenancy in common
    B.   Tenancy in entirety
    C.   Tenancy in sufferance
    D.   Ownership in severalty

39. Can a salesperson hold other jobs?

    A.   Yes
    B.   No
    C.   Only if it is in real estate
    D.   Maybe

40. What does the Secondary Mortgage Market refer to in the loan process?

    A.   Buyers that buy houses on mortgage
    B.   Sellers that offer buy down arrangement
    C.   Lending market
    D.   Private investors and government agencies that buy and sell real estate mortgages

41. What are air rights?

   A.   Right to breath
   B.   Right to own an airspace
   C.   Right to package air
   D.   Rights granted to a property owner on the vertical space above the property

42. What is the relationship where agents work together in the best interest of their respective clients?

   A.   Dual agency
   B.   Single agency
   C.   Co-broking
   D.   Co-borrowing

43. What is the legal term for passing responsibility of your apartment onto another tenant?

   A.   Sub lease
   B.   Lease assignment
   C.   Leasehold
   D.   Lease break

44. If you have a loan of $200,000 with a 12% interest, how much do you pay in interest every month?

   A. $1,200
   B. $2,000
   C. $2,400
   D. $24,000

45. What are the extra charges above the selling costs that are incurred by the buyer on the purchase of a home?

   A.   Common costs
   B.   Closing costs
   C.   Down payment
   D.   Short fall

46. What are the monthly charges imposed on condo tenants?

   A.   Common charges
   B.   Common costs
   C.   Service fees
   D.   Short fall

47. What is the name given to the ratio defined by dividing monthly debt payments to gross monthly income?

   A.   Loan to value ratio
   B.   Debt to income ratio
   C.   Earnest money deposit
   D.   Foreclosure

48. What is the percentage amount of the selling price that is deposited by the buyer when closing a real estate transaction?

   A.   Down payment
   B.   Escrow
   C.   Earnest money deposit
   D.   Tax abatement

49. What is earnest money deposit?

    A.   Money deposited by the buyer to the seller to show interest in the purchase of a home
    B.   Purchase money
    C.   Down payment
    D.   Security deposit

50. What is the financial agreement that allows a third party to regulate payment where two parties are involved?

    A.   Security deposit
    B.   Sales deposit
    C.   Escrow
    D.   Earnest money deposit

51. What is the notice given when a tenant is in violation of the lease agreement and is up for eviction?

    A.   Notice to cure
    B.   Notice of intention
    C.   Notice of termination
    D.   Notice to quit

52. What is the notice given when a squatter is accommodated without the landlord's consent?

    A.   Notice of default
    B.   Notice of intention
    C.   Notice to cure
    D.   Notice to quit

53. What is the notice given to state that no work has been performed?

    A.   Notice of cessation
    B.   Notice given to evict an unruly tenant
    C.   Notice filed in court by a lender on defaulting of payment
    D.   Notice to discontinue the breach of lease within 10 days

54. What is the name given to a visit made to a potential property to identify the condition of the house?

    A.   Final walk through
    B.   Home inspection
    C.   Appraisal
    D.   Assessment

55. What mortgage plan allows a borrower to switch to a fixed-rate mortgage?

    A.   Adjustable Rate Mortgage
    B.   Convertible ARM
    C.   Fixed rate mortgage
    D.   Floating rate mortgage

56. What is the situation that arises when an individual that is legally required to make payments does not fulfill this obligation?

    A.   Delinquency
    B.   Defaulting
    C.   Escalation clause
    D.   Foreclosure

57. Which agency insures FHA-approved lenders?

A. CERCLA
B. Consumer Financial Protection Bureau
C. Federal Emergency Management Agency
D. Federal Housing Administration

58. Which agency is commissioned with overseeing products and services offered to consumers in the finance industry?

A. Consumer Financial Protection Bureau
B. Federal Housing Administration
C. Environmental Protection Agency
D. Federal Emergency Management Agency

59. What service allows brokers to share their listings?

A. Broker Listing Service
B. Single Agency Listing
C. Multiple Listing Service
D. Shared Listing Service

60. What is the contract covering household maintenance systems?

A. Deed
B. Home warranty
C. Hazard insurance
D. HO4

61. What is the name given to a real estate transaction where buyers outbid each other for the property?

A. Acceleration clause
B. Escalation clause
C. Public auction
D. Tender

62. What is the name given to a notice given showing interest in a property?

A. Notice of cessation
B. Notice to cure
C. Notice of default
D. Notice of intent

63. What is the increase in the value of a property?

A. Appreciation
B. Depreciation
C. Obsolescence
D. All of the above

64. What is the mortgage payment plan that involves making payments every fortnight?

A. Balloon mortgage
B. Biweekly mortgage
C. Blanket mortgage
D. Graduated mortgage

65. What term is used to describe the document attached to an original contract?

    A. Addendum
    B. Signed agreement
    C. Requirements clause
    D. Terms and conditions

66. What refinancing method allows a borrower to acquire cash from the transaction?

    A. Cash flow
    B. Cash out refinance
    C. Cash on cash return
    D. Refinancing

67. Who oversees that code restrictions are followed and construction / renovation are done by licensed professionals?

    A. Contractor
    B. Department of Buildings
    C. Zoning board
    D. Architectural Review Board

68. What is the final stage of a real estate transaction?

    A. Closing
    B. Sale
    C. Final walk through
    D. Handing of the title

69. What is the percentage of the selling price that is usually earned by a real estate agent for facilitating the transaction?

    A. Bonus
    B. Commission
    C. Salary
    D. Rent

70. What is the name of fees paid to the lender at closing in exchange for a reduced interest rate?

    A. Mortgage
    B. Service fee
    C. Discount points
    D. Principal fee

71. Which Act was passed to protect against discrimination in borrowing?

    A. Equal Credit Opportunity Act
    B. Fair and Accurate Credit Transaction Act of 2003
    C. The Fair Credit Reporting Act
    D. Truth in Lending Act

72. What does the phrase "For Sale by Owner" mean?

    A. A sale is being facilitated by an agent
    B. Investors are open to receiving offers
    C. A property sale is being handled without a real estate agent
    D. All of the above

Practice Test 4

73. What is the name of the document used to summarize all the fees incurred by the lender and borrower during settlement of a loan?

A. Financial statement
B. Invoice
C. IOU
D. Settlement statement

74. Which entity determines the assessed value of a property?

A. Building Inspector
B. Municipal council
C. Real estate agent
D. Tax assessor

75. If a property is taxed at 40% with a tax levy of $88,000, what is its assessed value?

A. $220,000
B. $146,666
C. $123,200
D. None of the above

76. Which type of estate has rights to the property for an indefinite duration?

A. List estate
B. Estate for years
C. Freehold estate
D. Less-than-freehold estate

77. Which of the following is **not** an essential element of a deed?

A. Signature of the grantee
B. Date
C. Identification of the grantor and grantee
D. Adequate description of the property

78. What is a lessor?

A. A person who leases real estate property from the owner of said property
B. A person that makes a grant
C. The owner of real estate who leases the property to another
D. The person who transfers property by sale

79. What is the definition of a joint tenancy?

A. When property is held by two or more parties
B. When a third-party trust owns the property
C. When the seller and the buyer both own the property
D. When the property is inherited by a family member

80. What is the definition of a trust deed?

A. The owner of the real estate property who leases the property to another
B. A deed with limited or no warranties
C. A deed that transfers property to a family member
D. A document used when one party has taken out a loan from another party to purchase property

81. _____ refers to land and buildings that need to be held for a long period of time to pay for themselves.

    A. Fixity
    B. Nonhomogeneity
    C. Situs
    D. Datum

82. A shop owner leases a space in a strip mall for 2 years. The strip mall is sold to a new owner during the duration of the lease. What is the status of the lease?

    A. The lease is void
    B. The new property owner and tenant must honor all the terms of the original lease
    C. The new property owner has the right to make changes to the lease within 30 days of the sale
    D. The lease starts fresh with the new property owner as the landlord

83. A homeowner's association does not allow owners to have pets. This is an example of a _____ clause.

    A. Possessions
    B. Contingency
    C. Restricted covenants
    D. Defeasance

84. Tenancy by the entirety is only applicable to _____.

    A. Homeowners with an FHA loan
    B. Low income homeowners
    C. Recently divorced couples
    D. Married couples

85. A building inspector must provide a(an) _____ before the property can be used.

   A. Certificate of occupancy
   B. Quitclaim deed
   C. Pre-qualification
   D. Examination of title

86. Which of the following is a type of zoning?

   A. Rural
   B. Business
   C. Vacation
   D. Landmark

87. A _____ is a real estate professional that performs a visual survey of a property's structure.

   A. Developer
   B. Broker
   C. Real estate appraiser
   D. Home inspector

88. Which of the following is an example of a special purpose real property?

   A. Farm
   B. Public school
   C. Timeshare
   D. Condominium

89. _____ is the 2nd largest purchaser of the secondary market and buys mainly FHA and VA loans.

   A. Federal National Mortgage Association
   B. U.S. Housing and Urban Development
   C. Government National Mortgage Association
   D. Federal Housing Administration loan

90. Which of the following is not an economic characteristic of land?

   A. Scarcity
   B. Permanence of investment
   C. Size
   D. Improvements

91. A _____ is a provision in a mortgage that can make the debt immediately due if the borrower sells the property.

   A. Acceleration clause
   B. Alienation clause
   C. Prepayment clause
   D. Defeasance clause

92. Which survey system was adopted in 1785, and is also called the Public Land Survey System or Rectangular Survey System?

   A. Geographic Information System
   B. Tallahassee Meridian
   C. Government Survey System
   D. Principal Meridian

93. What is condemnation?

   A. The right the government has to acquire privately owned property for public use

   B. Occurs when the government seizes private property and compensates the owner

   C. Occurs when the government seizes private property and does not compensate the owner

   D. The right the government has to take privately owned property for private use

94. Which organization purchases conventional loans from savings and loans to promote stability and affordability in the housing market?

   A. Federal Home Loan Mortgage Corporation

   B. U.S. Housing and Urban Development

   C. Federal Housing Administration

   D. National Realtors Association

95. Which factors affect the demand of real estate?

   A. Population

   B. Employment

   C. Demographics

   D. All of the above

96. Which rights give the owner the right to access water when property is adjacent to a lake or an ocean?

   A. Littoral rights

   B. Riparian rights

   C. Quitclaim deed

   D. Easement

97. A _____ is a process that releases the borrower from the obligation of debt once all mortgage payment terms are met.

    A. Acceleration clause
    B. Defeasance clause
    C. Alienation clause
    D. None of the above

98. Also called restrictive covenants, this limits how a piece of real estate can be used.

    A. Reconveyance
    B. Zoning ordinances
    C. Deed restrictions
    D. Arbitration

99. Which legal document establishes one debt as inferior to another debt for collecting repayment from a debtor?

    A. Purchase agreement
    B. Closing disclosure
    C. Property deed
    D. Subordination agreement

100. Which law requires financial institutions to maintain, report and disclose loan information regarding mortgages?

    A. Home Mortgage Disclosure Act
    B. Community Reinvestment Act
    C. Real Estate Settlement Procedures Act
    D. Truth in Lending Act

101. The _____ is a law that regulates the design and improvements of a subdivision in the state of California.

    A.   New Development Act
    B.   California Subdivision Map Act
    C.   Subdivision Law
    D.   California New Development Act

102. In which of the following situations does title insurance not protect a buyer?

    A.   Incorrect signatures on a document
    B.   Ownership by another party
    C.   Zoning restrictions
    D.   Flawed records

103. Which statement is true about state and local property codes?

    A.   National codes prevail against state and local codes
    B.   Local codes are always stricter than state codes
    C.   The stricter of the two codes prevail
    D.   A&B only

104. Which statement is true about tenant occupancy in the state of California?

    A.   There are housing laws that restrict the number of people who can live in a unit
    B.   There can only be 2 people per 100 square feet in a rented place
    C.   There are no laws about how many people can live in a unit
    D.   Only the landlord decides these regulations

105. This law was established to ensure the availability of affordable housing and enforce regulations of housing and accessory buildings.

  A. Federal housing Laws
  B. State Housing Law
  C. DRE laws
  D. Cal-BRE Act

106. A living quarter that is on the same lot as a primary home is called a _____.

  A. Accessory Dwelling Units
  B. Multi-family home
  C. Primary Dwelling Unit
  D. Addition family unit

107. A material fact is information that concerns the _____ of property.

  A. Ceilings
  B. Floor insulation
  C. Roof
  D. All of the above

108. Which clause requires the borrower to pay the mortgage in full before transferring the property to another person?

  A. Acceleration clause
  B. Prepayment clause
  C. Alienation clause
  D. Transfer clause

109. This law is a consumer protection statute that ensures that adequate disclosures are made.

    A.   Subdivided Lands Act
    B.   Subdivision Map Act
    C.   Consumer Protection Laws
    D.   California Disclosure Law

110. Who is responsible for interpreting and enforcing the Subdivided Lands Act?

    A.   Attorney General
    B.   California Department of Real Estate
    C.   Real estate brokers
    D.   Local governments

111. What is the maximum amount of personal funds a broker can hold in an account to cover charges and not be guilty of commingling?

    A. $1,000
    B. $500
    C. $200
    D.   There is not maximum

112. The Real Estate Commission is responsible for creating an equal opportunity industry. In order to achieve this agent must _____.

    A.   Be free of bias
    B.   Know that race, creed and color are not material facts
    C.   Do unto others as you would have them do unto you
    D.   All of the above

113. If a subdivider sells half the lots to one buyer and options the remaining lots to another buyer, the subdivider must also _____.

  A. Notify the buyers of the sale
  B. Notify the Department of Real Estate
  C. They are not able to sell the lots separately
  D. They do not have to do anything

114. California realtors are required to adopt the _____ Code of Ethics.

  A. Brokerage's
  B. National Association of Realtors
  C. Their own
  D. They are not required to adopt any code of ethics.

115. A broker is required to retain records for how many years?

  A. 5 years
  B. 10 years
  C. 1 year
  D. 3 years

116. What is a notice of non-responsibility?

  A. When a tenant approves repairs without the landlord's consent
  B. When a seller states that they are not responsible for any repairs
  C. A document that protects a broker from any liability when showing a home
  D. A form filled out by a buyer to put responsibility of repairs on the previous owner

117. What is the difference between a covenant and a condition?

   A. A covenant is a promise and a condition is a contingency

   B. A condition only occurs in foreclosure sales

   C. A covenant is a contingency and a condition is a promise

   D. None of the above

118. A group of people who join together to invest in real estate is called a _____.

   A. Joint tenancy

   B. Tenancy in common

   C. Syndicate

   D. Group investment

119. A _____ provides a waiver from zoning requirements but does not change the zoning laws.

   A. Variance

   B. Subdivision

   C. Arbitration

   D. Blockbusting

120. What is a dominant tenant?

   A. A tenant who is in a lease to buy contract

   B. A tenant of property who also owns other property within that building

   C. A tenant who has precedence over another

   D. Land that benefits from an easement

121. Which of the following is true about deed restrictions?

    A. Limit how real estate can be used
    B. Prohibiting the sale of property to certain ethnic groups is illegal
    C. Limit what can be built on a piece of property
    D. All of the above

122. _____ is the land that the owner grants easement to the owner of another property.

    A. Dominant tenement
    B. Servient tenement
    C. Land sharing
    D. None of the above

123. Which type of lien is usually filed by contractors to seek unpaid compensation?

    A. Mechanic's lien
    B. Judgement lien
    C. Judicial lien
    D. General lien

124. A(n) _____ is when a landlord fails to act, and the tenant is forced to move out and terminate the lease.

    A. Constructive eviction
    B. Retaliatory eviction
    C. Uninhabitable eviction
    D. None of the above

125. A _____ allows the grantee peaceful possession of property without the fear of being ousted by a person with a superior claim to the property.

    A. Covenant of seisin
    B. Covenant against encumbrance
    C. Covenant of further assurance
    D. Covenant of quiet enjoyment

126. When does curable depreciation occur?

    A. When the cost of a repair is less than what the repair will add to the value of the property
    B. When the depreciation of property can be fixed
    C. When property increases in value instead of decreasing
    D. None of the above

127. This document contains an agreement to transfer ownership from one owner to another owner.

    A. Transfer of title
    B. Deed
    C. Transfer documents
    D. Property transfer forms

128. _____ are the traditional loan sources of savings and loans in the California mortgage market.

    A. Mortgage markets
    B. Federal mortgage banks
    C. Depository institutions
    D. None of the above

129. A _____ is an order that directs a person to stop committing an act that violates the Real Estate Law.

    A. Refrain order
    B. Desist and refrain order
    C. Cease order
    D. Desist order

130. A _____ is when a title transfer of real property occurs through a will.

    A. Devise
    B. Testament transfer
    C. Real property transfer
    D. Will property transfer

131. Counties in California have the right to impose this tax at the rate of 55 cents per $500 of property value.

    A. County tax
    B. Documentary transfer tax
    C. Local tax
    D. Property tax

132. _____ is a loss in property value because of factors outside of the property.

    A. Economic obsolescence
    B. Functional obsolescence
    C. Technological obsolescence
    D. Aesthetic obsolescence

133. This type of rent is set by the market instead of by the lease.

    A. Contract rent
    B. Profit rent
    C. Market rent
    D. Economic rent

134. This refers to crops that require annual planting by a tenant on the landlord's land.

    A. Business profit
    B. Agricultural profit
    C. Emblements
    D. None of the above

135. _____ is the extension of an improvement across a property boundary line onto another person's property.

    A. Redlining
    B. Encroachment
    C. Blockbusting
    D. Overlapping

136. An agent brings a willing and able buyer to a seller. This is called (a) _____.

    A. Ready buyer
    B. Principal
    C. Procuring cause
    D. None of the above

137. Which type of contract requires both parties to a contract to perform an act?

A. Express contract
B. Bilateral express contract
C. Lateral contract
D. Uniform contract

138. What is a fee simple subsequent?

A. An estate that cannot be taken even if a specific act is performed
B. An estate that can be taken if an act is performed
C. An estate that can only pass from parent to child
D. An estate that cannot be sold to specified persons

139. _____ is a note where the interest rate has the ability to change on the term of the loan.

A. Variant mortgage
B. Fixed rate mortgage
C. Adjustable rate mortgage
D. Both B&C

140. A built-in refrigerator is an example of which one of the five tests of a fixture?

A. Agreement between the parties
B. Relationship of the parties
C. Method of attachment
D. Adaptability

141. Which of the following is a type of severance?

    A.   Actual
    B.   Fixed
    C.   Alluvial
    D.   None of the above

142. Which of the following statements is true about water rights?

    A.   Rights follow an owner not the property
    B.   Water rights are appurtenant
    C.   Owners cannot use the water for anything but aesthetic purposes
    D.   All of the above

143. This protects a surviving spouse by prevent either spouse from passing property to someone else through a will.

    A.   Community property with a right of survivorship
    B.   Marital rights
    C.   Community property rights
    D.   Right of survivorship

144. Which of the following is not a principle of agency law?

    A.   Loyalty
    B.   Reasonable care
    C.   Commission
    D.   Obedience

145. _____ is the act of cultivating leads to generate business.

   A. Prospecting
   B. Cold calling
   C. Advertising
   D. Referral contacting

146. What is the definition of the term accretion?

   A. Land lost due to the changes in plots
   B. Land accumulated due to changes in plots
   C. Land lost by the gradual increase of water
   D. Land accumulated by the gradual subsiding of water

147. _____ exists if a party can learn certain facts through review of records located at the county office. Even if the party does not know about the records _____ still exists.

   A. Alluvial
   B. Constructive notice
   C. Actual notice
   D. Due diligence

148. Which of the following is a type of actual notice?

   A. Express
   B. Implied
   C. Noted
   D. Both A&B

149. What is an allodial title?

    A.   Property ownership free of any superior landowner

    B.   Ownership with 3 or more stakeholders

    C.   Property ownership with a superior landowner

    D.   Property ownership of a unit within a building

150. A promise to do whatever is reasonably necessary to help the grantee perfect a title in the future is called a _____.

    A.   Covenant of seisin

    B.   Covenant of further assurance

    C.   Covenant warranty

    D.   Covenant of no encumbrances

Answer Key

1.	D	31.	C	61.	B	91.	B	121.	D
2.	D	32.	D	62.	D	92.	C	122.	B
3.	B	33.	B	63.	A	93.	B	123.	A
4.	A	34.	B	64.	B	94.	A	124.	A
5.	D	35.	D	65.	A	95.	D	125.	D
6.	A	36.	B	66.	B	96.	A	126.	A
7.	D	37.	A	67.	B	97.	B	127.	B
8.	D	38.	C	68.	A	98.	C	128.	C
9.	B	39.	A	69.	B	99.	D	129.	B
10.	B	40.	D	70.	C	100.	A	130.	A
11.	A	41.	D	71.	A	101.	B	131.	B
12.	D	42.	C	72.	C	102.	C	132.	A
13.	B	43.	B	73.	D	103.	C	133.	D
14.	A	44.	B	74.	D	104.	A	134.	C
15.	B	45.	B	75.	A	105.	B	135.	B
16.	B	46.	A	76.	C	106.	A	136.	C
17.	C	47.	B	77.	A	107.	D	137.	B
18.	C	48.	A	78.	C	108.	C	138.	B
19.	D	49.	A	79.	A	109.	A	139.	C
20.	D	50.	C	80.	D	110.	B	140.	D
21.	B	51.	C	81.	A	111.	C	141.	A
22.	A	52.	D	82.	B	112.	D	142.	B
23.	B	53.	A	83.	C	113.	B	143.	A
24.	A	54.	B	84.	D	114.	B	144.	C
25.	B	55.	B	85.	A	115.	D	145.	A
26.	D	56.	A	86.	A	116.	A	146.	D
27.	A	57.	D	87.	D	117.	A	147.	B
28.	A	58.	A	88.	B	118.	C	148.	D
29.	C	59.	C	89.	C	119.	A	149.	A
30.	C	60.	B	90.	C	120.	D	150.	B

1.   **D) All of the above**

Commercial property includes mixed use buildings (e.g. retail store on the first floor, residences above) office buildings, hotels, retail stores, multifamily houses, industrial warehouses, and more.

2.   **D) Steering**

Steering is the act of guiding prospective buyers to specified settlement areas based on race, religion and other discriminatory factors.

3.   **B) Net lease**

This is a lease where the tenant pays rent and part of utilities fee and property taxes. The landlord is tasked with paying the utility bills and property taxes that are not covered by the tenant. This lease is common in commercial real estate.

4.   **A) Lis Pendens**

This is a legal notice that a lawsuit concerning a real estate property is pending. Usually involves a property title or claims of ownership interest. Details of a property whose title is in question are required to be filed at the county record to notify future buyers and lenders.

5.   **D) Zoning Board of Appeals**

The Zoning Board of Appeals is a board of select members that is given jurisdiction to hear and decide on appeals regarding zoning laws.

6.   **A) Mortgage Banker**

A mortgage banker is an individual who originates, closes and funds with his own funds or that of a company. Once a mortgage is originated it is either retained or sold to an investor. A mortgage banker has the power to approve or reject a mortgage and earns fees on the origination of a loan.

7.   **D) Sheathing**

Sheathing is a covering structure and acts as a case for the exterior of the home. Usually used to describe a boarding material that forms the roof, floor and walls. It provides a surface for other materials and strengthens weather resistance.

8.   **D) Landlord**

A security deposit is an amount equaling monthly rent that is paid to ensure rent will be paid and to cater for other responsibilities highlighted in the lease. Can also be used as security for unpaid rent and damages and is held onto by the landlord.

9. **B) Effective age**

This is an estimate of a building age based on its utilities and the wear and tear. It could be the actual age or a little more or less than the actual age. This is dependent on maintenance, remodeling and removal of inadequacies. It is used to determine the remaining life of a building.

10. **B) Three years**

Brokers are required by law to hold on to a copy of property files for a minimum of 3 years. This is to act as a proof in case of a dispute in the future. These include copies of all listings, deposit receipts, cancelled checks and trust records executed or obtained during the transaction.

11. **A) British Thermal Unit**

Defined as the amount of heat required to raise the temperature of one pound of water by one-degree Fahrenheit. In the case of air conditioning, it is defined as the number of BTU per hour products that can be added or removed from the air.

12. **D) Habendum clause**

This is a legal agreement that involves the rights and interests of a property being transferred to a lessee. For a leased property there is a transfer of ownership and restrictions on the property. A purchased property is void of restrictions and only transfers ownership.

13. **B) Passive**

This is an income source that requires little to no daily input in order to yield returns.

14. **A) Ground lease**

This is a lease agreement where a tenant is allowed to develop a parcel of land during the lease period. On expiry of the lease, all improvements remain in the owner's custody. Land leases are often last between 50-99 with other agreement allowing for renewal.

15. **B) Building codes**

These are a set of regulations that are put in place to ensure design, construction, alteration and maintenance of structures is done according to the state's requirements. They aim at safeguarding the health, safety and welfare of the occupants.

16. **B) $335,051**

$325,000 / (1 - 0.03) = $335,051

17.   **C) A fixture**

A fixture is any physical property that is permanently attached to real property (usually land). Fixtures are treated as a part of real property. Examples of fixtures are ceiling fans and TV mounts.

18.   **C) Offsite improvements**

Offsite improvements are amenities that are not within the premise of the structure but are necessary to maximize the use of the property and ultimately increase the value of the property.

19.   **D) Joint tenancy**

Joint tenancy is a form of ownership in which several people own a property together, each with equal shares and rights. If one of the owners in a joint tenancy dies, that owner's share in the property is automatically passed to the remaining owners.

20.   **D) Preventive maintenance**

In order to maintain tenants and an acceptable return on an investment, routine checks and repairs have to be done. These are done to safeguard against failing which may incur losses to the property manager that arise due to cost of replacement.

21.   **B) CERCLA**

The Comprehensive Environmental Response Compensation and Liability Act of 1980 was enacted in order to identify, investigate and facilitate cleanup of hazardous sites. The act is currently administered by the Environmental Protection Agency.

22.   **A) A shared tenancy in which each holder has a distinct, separately transferable interest**

This type of ownership is characterized by ownership between two or more people who can have either equal or unequal shares. Unlike a joint tenancy, if an owner dies, the person's share is passed to his/her heirs and not distributed to the remaining owners.

23.   **B) Cash flow**

This is the amount of profit retained after paying off all operating costs and repurposing amounts made in dividends for use in future repairs. To be able to profit from an investment, one must maintain a positive cash flow.

24.   **A) A lien that arises without the property owner's consent**

Involuntary liens are placed by government facilities for unpaid taxes.

25. **B) Homestead property**

Homestead laws are laws that exist to ensure to protect owners from losing their home equity while filing for bankruptcy. Homestead property enables an individual to declare a portion of property as homestead to avoid forced sale.

26. **D) Special agent**

This is an agent engaged to perform a specific duty for a client. Their authority is limited to that particular task that translates in the expiry of the contract once the task is completed.

27. **A) Bundle of rights**

These are legal rights that are granted to a property buyer which include right to possession, control, exclusion, enjoyment and disposition. A property owner is automatically granted the bundle of rights. In a commercial property, different rights can be assigned to different parties.

28. **A) $1,000**

Violation of license laws may result in suspension of a license or a fine of not more than $1,000 paid to the Department of State. A reprimand is given together with the fine.

29. **C) 39 years**

After 39 years a commercial property is eligible for applying for value loss by depreciation in order to reduce property taxes levied

30. **C) Proration**

Proration occurs during corporate action to ensure all shareholders are treated fairly and a company does not deviate from its original target. Shareholders are offered equity or cash and required to elect one. Once the election is done, shareholders are compensated and if the shares or cash are not enough to satisfy the election each shareholder gets their due in both equity and cash.

31. **C) 7.48 gallons**

32. **D) Operating statement**

An operating statement is a financial statement that is done monthly and annually to document the expenses incurred and revenue gained. From the statement one can calculate the net profit or loss within the period.

33. **B) Condop**

This is a real estate building where the housing units are divided into co-op residential units and condos. They offer more flexible rules than a co-op. Condo units are retained or sold separately by the developer.

34. **B) General Agent**

This is an agent that is mandated to represent the principal in more than one affair.

35. **D) Usury**

These are laws that are laws set in place to protect borrowers from abusive lending such as imposing unusually high interest rates. Lenders usually target with little knowledge on the traditional loan system. An APR is usually set to protect buyers from being exploited by lenders.

36. **B) Leasehold**

This is a title on a property being leased and scheduled payments are made throughout the term of the lease. Improvements made within the property are either expensed or capitalized depending on their values.

37. **A) Mortgage**

A mortgage is a voluntary lien taken out to raise funds to buy a property. The lien is entered willingly and therefore possession of the property remains with the debtor.

38. **C) Tenancy in sufferance**

In this case, a tenant is granted the privilege to live within the premise before landlord decides to ask the tenant to vacate. Terms of the original lease must be met during this period of time. This type of tenancy can only be terminated by a written notice given not less than 30 days before the tenant is expected to move out.

39. **A) Yes**

There are no laws restricting a real estate salesperson from working multiple jobs.

40. **D) Private investors and government agencies that buy and sell real estate mortgages**

This is where home loans and servicing rights are bought within the market. Once a home loan is obtained, it is underwritten, financed and services by a lending facility. A lending facility sells loans to the secondary mortgage market in order to replenish loaning money.

41. **D) Rights granted to a property owner on the vertical space above the property**

The air space is subject to reasonable use by neighboring buildings and aircrafts. Like with property, air rights can be leased or sold.

42. **C) Co-broking**

This is a situation where two or more agents that are involved in the same the same transaction agree to work together in order to meet the needs of both parties. In this case, the agents are legally required to act in the best interest of the clients.

43. **B) Lease assignment**

A lease assignment is a legal arrangement where the landlord allows a tenant to assign another tenant to lease the apartment. The tenant is responsible for paying rent and utility fees directly to the landlord. In the case of a lease assignment, the previous tenant is held accountable for defaults in unpaid bills by the assignee.

44. **B) $2,000**

($200,000 * 0.12) / 12 = $2,000

45. **B) Closing costs**

These are the extra costs that are usually incurred by a home buyer on top the agreed upon price. They usually include title insurance, attorney fees and lender fees. These costs are negotiable but commonly paid by buyers.

46. **A) Common charges**

These are the monthly charges that are imposed on condo and condop tenants to cover common charges and amenities. They are usually cover maintenance of shared spaces and operation expenses of a building.

47. **B) Debt to income ratio**

This is a way lenders use to calculate the ability of a borrower to manage the monthly payments required in the settlement plan. Borrowers with a higher ratio have been established to experience struggles in meeting the monthly payments. 43% has been determined to be the highest ratio that can be offered credit.

48. **A) Down payment**

A down payment is an amount paid by the buyer to the seller to secure the property. A down payment is usually paid from the buyer's savings. Contrary to common belief, there is no set percentage of down payment that should be placed on a property

49. **A) Money deposited by the buyer to the seller to show interest in the purchase of a home**

This amount is deposited to give the buyer time to look into the title, sanction an appraisal and conduct an inspection of the property. This money can be returned to the buyer only in the case of a contract breach.

50. **C) Escrow**

This arrangement involves a third party that is neutral to the transaction. Usually used to secure payment in an account that can only be released on meeting of all the terms of the agreement. An escrow account is often used in transactions that involve large amounts of money such as real estate. A listing agent open an account and once the terms are signed upon by both the buyer and the seller, the deal is closed.

51. **C) Notice of termination**

This is a notice given to a tenant to end tenancy stating the reason for termination of tenancy, the date by which the tenant is required to vacate the premise and the legal implication of refusing to move.

52. **D) Notice to quit**

This is a notice given by the landlord regarding someone living in the home as a squatter. The notice usually states that the tenant is required to vacate the property within 10 days and the implications of failing to do so.

53. **A) Notice of cessation**

This is notice given by the contractor by the contractee to state that no work regarding construction has been done for a specified period of time. This notice is given in order to begin mechanical liens compensation.

54. **B) Home inspection**

They are an important part of the real estate transaction as one is able to identify the condition of the property being bought. Inspection of facilities such as plumbing, fixtures and foundation condition comes in handy in determining the value of the property.

55. **B) Convertible ARM**

This is a mortgage plan that allows an individual to benefit from the falling interest rates with the option of switching to a fixed-rate payment plan at a small fee. This switch can be made within the second to fifth year of the mortgage payment period.

56. **A) Delinquency**

This is a situation that arises where a borrower that is legally bound with the responsibility to make necessary payments on a loan or a bond interest foregoes paying the loan. Delinquency usually results in penalties depending on the type of loan and reasons behind failed payments.

57. **D) Federal Housing Administration**

This is United States Agency whose goal is to enable low income individual acquire mortgage loans. The agency approves and insures the lenders. An FHA loan requires a loan down payment and a credit score of at least 580.

58. **A) Consumer Financial Protection Bureau**

This is a regulatory agency that is tasked with the responsibility of overseeing the products and services offered to consumers by financial institutions. In the event of mishandling of a consumer, a complaint is filed to the CFPB for resolution.

59. **C) Multiple Listing Service**

This is a system employed by real estate broker that allows them to view each other's listings. Sharing the database amongst a group of brokers enables brokers to identify buyers for properties they are engaged in.

60. **B) Home warranty**

This is a contract made to ensure the cost of maintaining a household are met. It is put in place as a legal assurance that the property is fit for its intended purpose and meets the expectations of the buyer. It is usually taken to protect against expensive home repairs.

61. **B) Escalation clause**

This is a contract that allows a buyer to set a selling price but any offers higher than the stated price will automatically lead to an increase in the set price. This gives sellers an option to outbid each other and help in making the decision for the sale price.

62. **D) Notice of intent**

This is a non-binding proposal between a buyer and seller of a property to negotiate terms of a real estate transaction. It is usually detailed and lays key points on the weight of the transaction. It is usually used to determine the seriousness of the prospective buyer on the property.

63. **A) Appreciation**

This is the increase in the value of an asset over a period of time. It usually occurs due to increased demand or weakening supply.

64. **B) Biweekly mortgage**

This is a mortgage that requires a principal and interest payment plan every two weeks. It usually has a reduced interest rate throughout the lifespan of the loan.

65. **A) Addendum**

This is an attached document that is usually included as part of the contract during the preparation. It can act as an informal explanatory attachment or to indicate other requirements of the contract that have not been included in the main attachment.

66. **B) Cash out refinance**

This is where a homeowner refinances a mortgage for more than its value and withdraws the difference amount as cash. It is only possible to borrowers with a 20% equity on their mortgage.

67. **B) Department of Buildings**

In order to ensure that building codes are adhered to and construction and renovations are done by professionals, a building permit is required for any building or renovation project. A building permit is a go ahead issued by local government to a contractor to construct or remodel a building. It is issued to ensure that building codes are adhered to and standards are maintained.

68. **A) Closing**

This is the final stage of a real estate transaction. At this point, the date where contract becomes active is agreed on. On the closing date, the property is legally transferred from the seller to the buyer.

69. **B) Commission**

This is the percentage earned by a real estate agent for effort placed in facilitating the transaction. It is usually between 5-6% of the sales price and is paid by the seller on closing. It is usually split between the buyer's and seller's agent.

70. **C) Discount points**

Also referred to as mortgage points, these are fees paid directly to a lender by a homebuyer at closing time. They are usually paid in exchange for lower interest rates reducing monthly payments on the mortgage.

71. **A) Equal Credit Opportunity Act**

This act was enacted in 1974 and rules it unlawful for lenders to discriminate against loan applicants based on gender, race, age and religion.

72. **C) A property sale is being handled without a real estate agent**

This phrase is used to declare that a property sale is being handled without a real estate agent. While using real estate agents to facilitate sale, some home sellers would rather avoid agents in order to save on the amount spent on commission. In this case the seller must disclose that they are not using an agent.

73. **D) Settlement statement**

This is a document that is usually used to summarize expenses incurred during a loan translation and varies according to loan types. It is usually part of the closing package that must be reviewed and signed by the borrower when closing a loan. A comprehensive settlement statement is legally required for every loan.

74. **D) Tax assessor**

An official whose responsibility is to determine the value of each taxable property in a region.

75. **A) $220,000**

$88,000 / 0.4 = $220,000

76. **C) Freehold estate**

An estate that has exclusive rights of the property for an undefined length of time. The three types of freehold estates are fee simple absolute, fee simple defeasible and life estate.

77. **A) Signature of the grantee**

The grantee does not need to sign a deed. A deed needs to be in writing, must be signed by the grantor, the grantor must have the legal capacity to transfer the property, the grantor and grantee must be identified, the property must be described adequately, the deed must be legally delivered to the grantee and the grantee must accept the deed.

78. **C) The owner of real estate who leases the property to another**

A person who grants a lease to someone else. This person is the owner of the real estate and leases it a lessee through an agreement.

79. **A) When property is held by two or more parties**

It is an agreement in which two or more people own a property with equal rights and obligations. Joint tenancy is typically entered at the same time and through a deed. If one of the owners were to die their portion of the property would automatically pass to the survivors.

80. **D) A document used when one party has taken out a loan from another party to purchase property**

It represents an agreement between the borrower and the lender in which the property is held in a trust managed by a third party until the borrower pays off the loan. The legal title of the property is transferred to the third party to hold. Trust deeds are used in place of mortgages in numerous states.

81. **A) Fixity**

Also called investment permanence is property that takes a long time to pay for itself. It also refers to the fact that land cannot be moved but is in a fixed location.

82. **B) The new property owner and tenant must honor all the terms of the original lease**

Property sold with an existing lease is still valid and it must be honored by both the new owner and the tenant.

83. **C) Restrictive covenants**

Restrictive covenants are restrictions on land used to ensure the value and enjoyment of adjoining land will be preserved. This clause limits what a tenant or owner can do with property.

84. **D) Married couples**

Tenancy by the entirety is a type of concurrent estate in real property limited to married couples. Each spouse has an equal and undivided interest in the property and they mutually own the entire estate.

85. **A) Certificate of occupancy**

A building inspector must issue a certificate of occupancy after the final inspection. It is a document issued by the local government or building department that states the building is in compliance with the building codes and is suitable for occupancy.

86. **A) Rural**

There are numerous different types of zoning: rural, residential, commercial, industrial, agricultural, combination and historic.

87. **D) Home inspector**

A home inspector determines the condition of the structure. A home inspection is a non-invasive examination of the home condition and should not be confused with an appraisal which determines the value of the property.

88. **B) Public school**

Public schools are an example of special purpose property. It is property that is appropriate for one type of use and has a unique design. It uses special construction materials and other features which limit the use of the property.

89. **C) Government National Mortgage Association**

The GNMA guarantees the timely payment of principal and interest on mortgage-backed securities that have been issued by approved lenders. It is also referred to as Ginnie Mae.

90. **C) Size**

Size is not an economic characteristic of land. The economic characteristics of land are factors that affect its value in the marketplace. These are scarcity, improvements, performance of investment and location.

91. **B) Alienation clause**

This clause states that the borrower needs to pay the mortgage in full before the borrower can transfer the property to another person. This clause will go into effect whether the property is transferred voluntarily or involuntarily.

92. **C) Government Survey System**

This system identifies reference lines and makes up townships and sections. It has been applied to most of the land in the United States since its adoption in 1785.

93. **B) Occurs when the government seizes private property and compensates the owner**

Condemnation occurs when the government acquires land through eminent domain. Eminent domain is the right the government has to acquire privately owned property for public use.

94. **A) Federal Home Loan Mortgage Corporation**

This organization was created by the congress but is not a government agency and does not receive government funding. It is owned by shareholders and overseen by its board of directors.

95. **D) All of the above**

The factors that affect demand are population, demographics, employment interest rates and borrowing costs.

96. **A) Littoral rights**

These rights are considered water rights that concern bodies of water that are static like an ocean, lake or bay. Rights for flowing water are determined by the riparian rights.

97. **B) Defeasance clause**

This clause states that a borrower will be given the title to the property once the mortgage payment terms are met. It is the final procedures in a mortgage contract.

98. **C) Deed restrictions**

Deeds restrictions are a clause in a deed that limits how real estate can be used and what can be built on the land. Most often the restrictions are not covered by community zoning regulations.

99. **D) Subordination agreement**

This agreement comes up when a home has a first and a second mortgage and the borrower would like to refinance the first mortgage. It adjusts the priority of the new loan.

100. **A) Home Mortgage Disclosure Act**

This law is used to monitor the geographic targets of mortgage lenders, provides mechanisms for predatory lending practices and provides reporting statistics on the mortgage market to the government.

101. **B) California Subdivision Map Act**

This act is used to regulate and control the design and improvement of subdivisions. It considers their relation to adjoining areas, requires the sub-dividers to install streets and other improvements and prevents fraud and exploitation.

102. **C) Zoning restrictions**

A title insurance protects a property owner and a lender against loss or damage that occurs due to liens, encumbrances or defects in the title. It protects against claims for past occurrences.

103. **C) The stricter of the two codes prevail**

These codes set a minimum standard that needs to be met by all housing, new and existing, to protect the residents. They are also called property maintenance codes or sanitation codes.

104. **A) There are housing laws that restrict the number of people who can live in a unit**

Housing laws are not hard and fast but in the past California law adopted a two-plus-one rule which stated two people per bedroom plus one additional person.

105. **B) State Housing Law**

The SHL is a program that has been established to ensure the availability of affordable housing and statewide regulations that protect the health, safety and general welfare of the public and occupants.

106. **A) Accessory Dwelling Units**

The ADU are living quarters on the same lot as a primary dwelling unit. California law has ways to increase this type of development.

107. **D) All of the above**

All of the above is true about material facts. It also includes information about windows, doors, foundation, driveways, sidewalks, fences, electrical and plumbing systems and another structural component. It's the things that concerns part of the property that may affect the value, desirability or ability to be used,

108. **C) Alienation clause**

This clause is in a mortgage contract that states that a borrower has to pay the mortgage fully prior to the borrower transferring the property to another person.

109. **A) Subdivided Lands Act**

This law is a consumer protection statute that ensures adequate disclosures are made. It regulates the public offerings of land in subdivision for sale or lease.

110. **B) California Department of Real Estate**

The DRE is required to interpreted and enforced the Subdivided Lands Act and the Commissioner is concerned with the financing and marketing arrangements.

111. **C) $200**

To avoid commingling a broker can only hold $200 dollars. Commingling occurs when there is a breach of trust and the fiduciary mixes funds that make it difficult to determine which funds belong to who.

112. **D) All of the above**

The Commissioner is responsible for creating an equal opportunity industry. In order to do so the agents must do all of the listed.

113. **B) Notify the Department of Real Estate**

The Department of Real Estate must be notified that there is a material change which occurs when the sub-divider sells the lots to two different buyers.

114. **B) National Association of Realtors**

The NAR code of ethics must be adopted by the California realtors. The NAR is a trade association that represents 14 million members.

115. **D) 3 years**

Brokers need to keep records for 3 years in California. These include listings, deposits, canceled checks, trust records and other document they executed or obtained for real estate transaction purposes.

116. **A) When a tenant approves repairs without the landlord's consent**

This document protects owners from liability for nonpayment of services done to their property. It needs to be recorded and posted within 10 days after the owner learns of the improvement.

117. **A) A covenant is a promise and a condition is a contingency**

A covenant is a promise to do something and a condition is a contingency that needs to be met or else a property can be gained or lost.

118. **C) Syndicate**

Investors pool their money to invest in a property that they would not have been able to on their own.

119. **A) Variance**

A variance allows property owners to deviate from zoning requirements. It allows owners to use their land in a way that would not be ordinarily permitted.

120. **D) Land that benefits from an easement**

A dominant tenant is land that benefits from easement. It is a parcel of real property that has an easement over another piece of property.

121. **D) All of the above**

All of the above is true, a deed restriction cannot stop a property from being sold to someone due to their ethnicity. Developers may include restrictions that are not covered by community zoning regulations.

122. **B) Servient tenement**

This is different than dominant tenement because a servient tenement is the party that grants the benefit or suffering of the burden.

123. **A) Mechanic's lien**

A mechanic's lien reserves the rights of the flier to seek unpaid compensation. These types of liens are usually filed by contractors or subcontractors.

124. **A) Constructive eviction**

This type of eviction occurs when the tenant is forced to move out because the landlord failed to act, i.e. the landlord refuses to provide heat to the apartment.

125. **D) Covenant of quiet enjoyment**

The covenant promises the grantee or tenant the right to undisturbed use and enjoyment of real property. The tenant or landowner has the right to possess the property in peace without disturbance.

126. **A) When the cost of a repair is less than what the repair will add to the value of the property**

A curable depreciation is a loss in value that can be corrected and is economically feasible. The cost to fix the issue is less than the loss in value so it makes economic sense to fix the problem.

127. **B) Deed**

This is a legal instrument to transfer ownership of real property from the grantor to the grantee. It was historically transferred through an act known as livery of seisin.

128. **C) Depository institutions**

Depository institutions are the traditional loan source. They are financial institutions in the United States such as a savings bank, commercial bank or credit union.

129. **B) Desist and refrain order**

This order states that a person needs to stop committing an act that is in violation with the Real Estate Law.

130. **A) Devise**

This is a gift of real property through a will or testament. It is also called a testamentary disposition of land or realty.

131. **B) Documentary transfer tax**

This California tax is 55 cents per $500 of property value or consideration paid. It allows counties to impose this tax.

132. **A) Economic obsolescence**

This type of loss in property value is changes in competition or surrounding land use. It is also called an external obsolescence.

133. **D) Economic rent**

This type of rent is the amount of rent that provides an adequate return on development cost. It is the excess profit.

134. **C) Emblements**

In the case of emblements, crops are treated as the tenant's personal property and not the landowner's. The tenant is still entitled to finish raising and harvesting crops even if the tenant has been evicted.

135. **B) Encroachment**

This occurs when an owner violates the property rights of their neighbor by building on or extending a structure onto the neighbor's land.

Practice Test 4 – Answers

136. C) Procuring cause

This can sometimes lead to a dispute with other agents. It is when the agent's efforts ultimately result in the sale of the property.

137. B) Bilateral express contract

This type of contract requires both parties to perform an action. The parties are the promisor and promise to perform an action in exchange for a promise to accept the offer for something valuable such as money

138. B) An estate that can be taken if an act is performed

This is similar to a fee simple but has a condition attached. I.e. if a piece of land is not used as a museum then the grantor can act against the grantee.

139. C) Adjustable rate mortgage

This type of mortgage has an interest rate that varies throughout the duration of the loan. It is also called an adjustable note.

140. D) Adaptability

Adaptability is an item that is integral to the home. A built-in refrigeration can be removed but it is a fixture because it is specific to a certain space. Flooring is another example of adaptability.

141. A) Actual

There are two types of severance actual and constructive. Actual severance is when an item is removed from the land and constructive severance is when an item has been detached by intent.

142. B) Water rights are appurtenant

This means that the rights are attached to the land and not the owner. An owner can use the water as they please as long as it does not harm upstream or downstream neighbors.

143. A) Community property with a right of survivorship

This is a hybrid of community property and right of survivorship rights. It also allows the surviving spouse the tax benefit of the double step-up.

144. **C) Commission**

An agent owes a principal the duty of loyalty, obedience and reasonable care. The agent must act in the best interest of the principal, must act reasonably within with scope that the principal provides and act rationally under the circumstances.

145. **A) Prospecting**

This involves sourcing new leads, leveraging social networks and engaging in the community to boost brand visibility.

146. **D) Land accumulated by the gradual subsiding of water**

Accretion is an increase of land because of the loss of water on a stream, lake or shoreline. It is a gradual gain of land because of the water that is subsiding.

147. **B) Constructive notice**

It is the presumption that a party has notice because it can be discovered through due diligence or inquiry into public records.

148. **D) Both A&B**

Express notice is when a person has been personally given notice about a property and implied notice is when a person has witnessed something that gives them information about the property.

149. **A) Property ownership free of any superior landowner**

An allodial title is when the owner has an absolute title over their real property. It is also referred to as allodial land.

150. **B) Covenant of further assurance**

This covenant states that the grantor will execute any documents needed by the grantee to fix defects in the grantee's title. This also means executing legal documents need by the grantee.

Resources

3.1 Finding a broker

Now that you've passed the exam, it's time to officially become an agent! Below is a list of companies and their websites to help you expedite your job search and help you start your journey in selling your first property!

Ackerman Realty Group – https://ackermanrealty.com
Alexandria Real Estate Equities – https://www.are.com
Allison James Estates & Homes – https://www.allisonjamesinc.com
CBRE Group – https://www.cbre.us
Digital Realty – http://www.digitalrealty.com
Equinix – http://www.equinix.com
Equity One Real Estate – http://tamikaellsworth.com
Essex Property Trust – https://www.essexapartmenthomes.com/en
Healthpeak Properties – https://www.healthpeak.com
J. Rockcliff Realtors – https://www.rockcliff.com
Keller Williams Realty – https://www.kwcalabasas.com
NextHome Town & Country – http://nexthometc.com
Pinnacle Estate Properties – https://www.pinnacleestate.com
Prologis – https://www.prologis.com
Public Storage – http://www.publicstorage.com

Re/Max Lakeside – http://lakearrowheadremax.com
Realty Income Corporation – https://www.realtyincome.com
Teles Properties – http://www.kristinhamm.com
Today Sotheby's International Realty – https://www.goldengatesir.com/eng
Whissel Realty Group – https://www.whisselrealty.com

3.2 Interviewing

Congratulations! You did get the interview. Now, just a little work and you can ace it!

First, start by going to all of the social media pages associated with your potential employer. Focus on several interesting things that they do and specialize in. Look at which type of listings they are showing on their pages and what types of neighborhoods they appear for listings. Look up the particular broker you are interviewing with and go to his/her LinkedIn page and learn more about her/him.

While you're looking at your potential employer's social media pages, take a look at your own. Are there any posts on your Facebook or other social media sites that need to be removed? Employers are looking at your pages. Anything inappropriate needs to go!

Real estate is all about creating a network of potential clients who trust that what you're selling to them will meet their needs. This means you must understand to differentiate between a client looking to buy a house to raise their newborn and a client who is looking for long term appreciation.

Try simulating cold calls by opening up random properties on Zillow or Trulia, studying them for 2 minutes, and then trying to sell your friend on these properties. They will most likely be asking similar questions to actual prospective buyers or sellers, so it's a very useful exercise in preparing yourself for the mock cold call during the interview.

In addition, study the geography of your broker's city to make sure you don't go in completely blind. Get familiar with the prices and trends in those areas and even take a tour. Drive or walk around and know the neighborhood like the back of your hand so you can impress the employer

On the day of the interview choose your outfit carefully. You should wear some type of suit and make sure your shoes are in good condition. Ask a friend to give you input on the clothes that make you look the most professional. Make sure you brushed your teeth, and your hair is neatly styled. Make sure you don't smell of smoke as most workplaces are smoke-free. No perfume or cologne – your new office may be perfume free. Never chew gum! You will not get the job!

When you arrive at the interview, always make sure to greet the receptionist. Every person you meet at your potential future employer is important! Make a good impression.

When you land the interview, it's important to have certain answers prepared to more commonly asked questions. First, let's look at general types of questions that you may be asked at any type of interview:

1. Tell me about yourself. This is not the time to talk about everything that happened to you from birth. This is an opportunity to show off a certain drive or characteristic or hobby that is special and helps to explain why you are seeking that particular job. For example, did you participate in a lot of team sports or a lot of clubs in high school or college? Did you work on volunteer projects that required you to meet a lot of new people of all ages and work with them and/or help them? The interviewer has your resume (Always bring extras with you!), so you do not have to spout off all of your previous education and positions. Devote just a sentence or two to that part of your answer.

2. What are your greatest strengths and weaknesses? This is a very tricky question. We all know our strengths; winning personality, gets along with everyone, good at math, good at negotiating, etc., but what about our weaknesses? Well, you certainly want to be honest but now isn't the time to confess all. Choose one. Do you take too long sometimes on a project because you want every detail to be perfect? Do you sometimes want to do something completely by yourself, but you really would be better off asking others for help? These are just two examples of weaknesses that won't sound like you are unprepared for your new job.

3. Where do you see yourself in 5 years? This seems pretty straightforward but be careful. The person interviewing you could be a manager. It is best not to say that you want his/her job. Instead, it may be better to say, I see myself expanding into new roles, doing what I do better, expanding my client base, becoming more successful, continuing my real estate education, and similar phrases.

4. Why did you choose our Company? Everyone asks this question. If you haven't gone to the Company's website, don't go to the interview. You should know everything about the Company and the local office where you are interviewing. You should know which type of real estate they specialize in, how long it's been in business, any recent mergers or expansions, the physical area it is licensed to practice in, and as much as you find on their website and Facebook page and other social media.

5. Why should I hire you and not the next person? This is your moment in the spotlight. Don't just say "pick me!!". Here is a sample: "All of my life, I have enjoyed working with people; when I worked at X company or volunteered at Y organization, I was able to get along with all types of people from children to the elderly. I also have been on teams or worked on teams, and I enjoy it greatly. I like to help people, and there is no bigger purchase than a home. I believe that I have the people skills and the real estate knowledge that I need to be a successful addition to your Company.

6. Why are you leaving your current job? This is not the moment to say how much you dislike your current manager or co-worker. Always be positive at your interview. You can talk about the lack of advancement opportunities, a salary freeze, future layoff being expected, change in your current employer's office location, or some other concrete reason. You can even say that you don't feel all of your skills are being utilized, and you want to use your new knowledge every day in your job.

7. Give me an example of a situation where you used teamwork to accomplish your goal. Even if you only work by yourself at your current job, look back to previous jobs and have the answer

ready. If you don't have a job that matches, think about your volunteer activities at your children's school or at a community center or retirement village.

8. Would you rather work by yourself or as part of a team? This may be a good one to answer with a bit of vagueness. You can say that it depends on what the assignment might be. Do you have to give a major presentation to a commercial client? That might be a great time to ask for input and help as needed. Do you have to write a simple analysis of a problem? Maybe you feel more comfortable completing this on your own. You might want to say that it is very important to ask for feedback from co-workers and managers on projects and on small assignments when you have questions or reach a dead end.

9. What type of manager do you prefer? Do you prefer to work independently or to have more direction? This is always a tricky one as well. Make sure, once again, that you don't diss any of your former managers. A good response would be that you expect some direction from your manager. You feel that you know generally when you need help and would be sure to ask your manager for direction at those times. Also, you welcome all constructive feedback. It is very important to show that you are open to learning and open to change.

10. Why do you have gaps on your resume? Make sure you know the answer in advance to this question. Were you raising a family, taking care of an elderly parent, moving across the country due to a partner relocation, volunteering, etc.? Whatever it is, make sure to answer this one without any hesitation and move on.

11. What is customer service? Be careful with this one. There are two types of customers – internal and external. Everyone you work with in your office is an internal customer; others are external. The same level of consideration should be given to both internal and external customers. Speak about how important it is to answer questions, do tasks that are needed, go above and beyond the average effort, and ask for help if you don't know the answers.

12. Are you organized? No one wants to admit they are disorganized. If you are going into real estate where there are mounds of paperwork and so many different elements to keep track with, let's assume that every person interviewing for this position must be organized!

13. What do you do when several people give you tasks to do, and it is clear to you that you will not be able to finish them on time?

14. Tell me about a time when you went above and beyond what was required? Hopefully, this will be an easy one to answer. Think about a suggestion you made to your manager to take on more work when a fellow employee was out sick or a time when you thought the presentation needed a special PowerPoint and you produced it.

15. Tell me about a time you had to deal with a difficult person and how you managed to diffuse the situation? You really need to think about this one in advance. If you can't think of a difficult person in your professional life, think about a friend of a friend or someone else. Always acknowledge a difficult person's feelings and avoid arguing about strong opinions that impact an issue that isn't really that important.

16. If we offer you the position, how much notice do you have to give to your current employer? Be prepared to know the answer to this one. If you say that you can leave tomorrow, your future employer may not be pleased. It shows that you are not being loyal to your current employer by leaving them in the lurch. Two weeks is standard practice, but if you have a contract, be sure to read it.

Then, you will be asked more specific questions that are relevant to the real estate industry or this particular job. These include but are not limited to:

1. Why do you want to work in the real estate business?
2. This is a commission-based business, which means there is no ceiling to how much you can earn, but it also means there is no floor either. Are you open to this?
3. Let's go through a mock cold call together. I'll be the buyer, and you'll be the seller's agent.
4. How would you sell a property in a neighborhood you've never been to before?
5. A couple is looking to buy their first home. What kind of houses would you suggest?
6. A seasoned investor is looking for investment properties. By coincidence, the Independence Hall is for sale and you are the seller's agent. Pitch it to them.
7. A retiree is looking to sell their house. He is unsure about whether it's a good time to sell it. Explain to them why it is a good time to put the property on the market.

Be prepared to answer technical questions you may have studied for your exam such as:

1. What is the difference between a joint tenancy and a tenancy by the entireties?
2. What is the difference between a cooperative and a condominium?
3. Why is title insurance important?
4. Why would a buyer agree to lease back to a seller?
5. What are the duties of a buyer's agent?
6. What is a tax credit opposed to a tax deduction?
7. What is an easement?
8. Why would someone want to partition property, and what does this mean?
9. When would there be a lien on real estate?
10. What happens at settlement?
11. Why would a homeowner agree to finance a second mortgage for the buyer?

At the end of an interview, the interviewer will always ask if you have any questions. It is never a good idea to say, "No"! Here are some suggestions:

1. If I work here full time, what would be a range of the commissions I could expect in the first year?
2. What type of commission structure is there? Are commissions paid immediately upon closing? What types of fees am I required to pay out-of-pocket? Do I pay any advertising, computer, or other fees?
3. How often would I normally be assigned floor duty? If I answer the phone while on floor duty, do I get that listing?
4. How many open houses would I normally attend a month?
5. What is your hiring process timewise?
6. Do you pay for continuing education?

7. Although I know there isn't a truly "typical" day, what kinds of activities will I be performing during my first few weeks on the job?
8. When I attend my first settlement, will someone more senior come with me to the closing?
9. Will I attend all of the inspections for my listings?
10. What are the types of problems that arise at settlement?
11. Do you give out a list of mortgage brokers to clients?
12. How many people work in this office?
13. Is there coordination with other nearby offices – both this brand and others?
14. Do you provide a list of mortgage brokers to the buyer?

When you are finished with your interview, make sure to thank the interviewer, ask for her/his card, and thank the receptionist before you leave. Every impression counts! When you arrive home, if you really do want to work at that office, within 24 hours write a short email thank you note to your interviewer. If you don't hear back within a week, you can send a brief follow-up e-mail expressing your continuing interest in the position.

Made in the USA
Las Vegas, NV
23 May 2021